Disciple Like Jesus
For Parents

Following Jesus' Method and Enjoying the Blessings of Children

By Alan Melton and Paul Dean

Endorsements for Disciple Like Jesus

" *Disciple Like Jesus* has the right idea. Their emphasis on parental discipleship is much needed, as we often seem to forget that one's own children provide the greatest opportunity and need for discipleship."

Dr. Christopher Cone, President, Tyndale
Theological Seminary

DISCIPLE LIKE JESUS FOR PARENTS is a must-read for every parent in America. In an age when Christians routinely lose their children to depravity by the end of college, Alan Melton and Paul Dean show us how to stop the trend. Their practical application of Biblical principles of discipleship to parenting can rescue an entire generation from disaster. I urge parents to read this book and pass it along to every parent you know.

Dr. Craig Bailey, Director, Buncombe
Baptist Association, Asheville, NC

"The present atmosphere in the United States and around the world demands that parents take up the call to actually engage in proactive parenting. *Disciple Like Jesus* has the compass pointed in the right direction. If you are convinced of the need to disciple your own child instead of hoping someone else will, *Disciple Like Jesus* offers much needed help."

Dr. Steve Spurlin, Pastor/Teacher, Viola
First Baptist Church

"*Disciple Like Jesus* has offered me encouragement and inspiration for following in the Master's footsteps, rather than trying to make my approach to discipleship up as I go along. It's a firm reminder that my service to the King is not about me, but about shining His light through my words and deeds so that others, specifically my children, will want a relationship with Him."

Deb Burton, Founder, Great Commission Family

"*Disciple Like Jesus* gets it. The key to reaching the world tomorrow is discipling our children today."

Rick Osborne, Best-Selling Christian Parenting Author

Contents

Personal Acknowledgements

This book has come in large part through a collaborative effort of many friends and family. I first want to thank my bride of 31 years, Donna, and my children Jennifer and Ryan! Thank you for sharing this vision with me, for teaching me, for your help with forming my thoughts and for editing this book.

Thanks be to God for those who serve on the Disciple Like Jesus ministry advisory board; Matt Chapman, Dr. Paul Dean, Isaac Fineman, Macky Pittman, Rev. Craig Reimer, Dr. Steve Rayburn, Dr. Keith Sherlin. I am especially thankful for Dr. Paul Dean who joined me to significantly improve the original manuscript and to generously co-author this book. Dr. Steve Rayburn made a significant contribution to this book and an even greater contribution in making a disciple out of me. Brian Byars recently joined our team and has been writing for us on Facebook. He did a fantastic job of designing the book cover. All of these men have influenced me and have played a significant role in writing this book. Over the past 37 years many others have been used of the Lord to shape my thoughts on discipleship; please forgive me if your name is not mentioned here.

Most of all I want to thank my Heavenly Father, who has been so merciful to make disciple out of me. The Lord gave me this burden approximately seven years ago, and then made the vision for the ministry clear in the summer of 2008. Praise the Lord for planting, watering and cultivating these ideas over the past few years.

Alan Melton, March 2009

This book bears witness to the grace of God powerfully at work in me and in the lives of my family members. He has increasingly moved me to seek to disciple like Jesus.

I am grateful to my precious wife, Mary, who has encouraged me to take that which God has given me and write it down. Her loving prompting was the primary impetus in me taking up the pen. Of course, to my three children, Jay, Christi, and Amy, I owe a debt of gratitude for giving me time that could have been spent with them to complete the manuscript for the sake of others.

To Alan Melton who invited me to participate with him in this project I cannot say thank you enough. The heart of the book is his and I am overwhelmed that he would allow me to work with him. My heart has been enlarged and my commitment has been deepened as a result of knowing and working with him here. Thank you again.

Ultimately, I am still amazed at God's grace and I am grateful to Him who counted me faithful and put me in the ministry though I was a rebel sinner without hope in this world. Moreover, He put individuals into my life who were willing to pour their lives into mine and disciple me. I can only do the same.

Paul J. Dean, March 2009

Foreword

We don't have to go far to find a great parenting book. In fact, there is an abundance of people willing to teach you how to parent better. But "great parenting" alone has yielded many of the poor results we see today. Alan Melton and Paul Dean have gotten it right. If we are to see young men and women who look like Christ, then we must disciple as Christ did. In *Disciple Like Jesus for Parents*, you'll be challenged to realize the death of "because I said so." Our children are reading our actions because they have been engineered by God to do so. Will they see Jesus or a detached set of beliefs you once held? Discipling our children is the longest running gig we'll have, we've got to get it right!

As a missionary to university students for years, it was my job to fill in the gaps left by the church and well-meaning parents who missed the mark. I can't express the number of college students I counseled who had grown up in a Christian home but had little to no understanding of what it meant to be a Christian. Their parents had hoped they would "just get it." Our children don't "just get it" they must be taught to follow Christ: that is they must be discipled. Discipleship is the parenting wave that is now! We've got to model for our children how to live Godly lives just as Jesus modeled it for those the Father entrusted to Him. Read *Disciple Like Jesus for Parents* and prepare to have a paradigm shift. Your children are depending on it.

Meeke Golden Addison
American Family Association
Mother of Moriah and Gabbi

Introduction

It was an all too familiar scene in the little country church. At the Wednesday night prayer meeting, Jack and Mary Johnson were on their knees. With tears and earnest pleading they prayed for their child. Since Emily, the younger of their two children, had left the nest to attend an excellent law school nearly four years ago, they had faithfully petitioned God for her return to the church.

With Mary at his side, Jack glanced up through his tears at the pew worn from hundreds of worshipers. It supported familiar items for worship: the Bible, the new hymnal, and the offering envelopes. The prayer list was lying on the floor. He quoted to himself, "Train up a child in the way he should go, and when he is old he will not depart from it" (Proverbs 22:6). How many times had he and Mary leaned on that verse? How many times had he prayed in this way? Was it now hundreds of times or perhaps even thousands? He thought about his youngest child Emily, born twenty-two years earlier, his "Sweetie." He remembered playing "patty cake," taking summer vacations together as a family, and their Sunday evening ritual picking up McDonald's on the way to church. Where had all the years gone?

As a successful pharmaceutical representative, Jack had provided well for his family. A two-story, 2800 square foot home in an upscale neighborhood, a boat and motorcycle parked in the garage, the very best colleges for his children, and a nice nest egg said as much. Yes, he had worked hard to provide. Weekly trips throughout the United States and abroad had filled his calendar but he was home some Saturdays and almost every Sunday. Of course, it seemed like the time was constantly fixed on fast forward on the weekends with various sports and extracurricular activities; church events and deacons meetings; planning sessions and teachers meetings. Jack's guilt about being away so much was somewhat placated by the fact that the whole family always looked forward to their summer vacations; they traveled to interesting if not exotic places and relished their time together; that is until the problems began.

The church pew creaked as he hugged his sobbing wife. Mary had a successful career as well in interior design and had been highlighted in numerous home and garden publications. She also served as Chair of the Cancer Society and had been busy juggling that service with her career in addition to shuttling her children to their various activities.

The problems came when Jack and Mary's children entered their teens. Adam, their oldest child, always had a chip on his shoulder. He didn't appreciate anything his dad did for him. He was always lost in his world of acid rock and MTV. When his dad confronted him, he exploded. Progressively, the explosions became louder until Adam ran out in a rage. The second page newspaper headline told the grim story; a head-on collision had claimed the lives of Adam and his companion.

Emily, a quiet child, gave them little trouble. She studied hard, was active in her youth group, and generally was low maintenance until her parents learned that at age fourteen she had had an abortion. The sixteen year old boyfriend that she had met at youth group seemed nice enough; his father was the pastor of their church. The boy had secretly transported Emily over the state line. After that event, Emily withdrew into a gothic world of depression and rebellion. Frankly, Jack was relieved when she finally went off to college to study law.

Jack and Mary had served the Lord faithfully since they had married nearly thirty years earlier. Jack had served in his church in virtually every role possible from bus driver to chairman of the deacons; Mary had been a Sunday School teacher for over twenty-five years. They had given over and above their tithe to support new buildings, new church plants, short term mission's trips, and youth events.

"How could the Lord have allowed this to happen to my family . . .?" Jack stopped himself mid sentence aware that his complaining was wrong. He dropped to his knees between the pews and could only groan as he sought comfort from the Holy Spirit. He quoted his favorite verse for what seemed like the millionth time, "Train up a child in the way he should go, and when he is old he will not depart." Jack was comforted to know that he had been faithful in taking his family to church and that someday Emily might return. Jack's and Amy's prayer vigil continues.

Consider the situation of Roger and Sheila: age forty-five and forty-four respectively. Roger owned a small business and Sheila was a secretary at a large company. They met at a church youth group meeting and began dating soon after. Married when they finished college, they were saddled with almost $40,000 in student-loan debt. Determined to obtain a piece of the "American Dream," they bought a home when their middle child Sarah was two years old. Over the years, they struggled to pay the bills. Roger worked seventy to eighty hours per week in his business while Sheila dropped the children off at a preschool program and a Christian school.

Roger and Sheila went through a mid-life crisis as Roger reached forty; he ran off with one of his sales staff and was absent from the family entirely for about ten months. The grace of the Lord drew him to repentance and he begged forgiveness from his family. However, Sheila had been taking long lunch breaks with her boss. She had fallen in love with him but soon realized after several secret rendezvous that the boss had no long term interest in the relationship. She and Roger struggled through these marital difficulties with the help of several Christian counselors.

By and large they neglected their children. Sure, they provided all their temporal needs and felt secure in the fact that they took them to church events. Chad was their pride and joy. He seemed to always rise above problems in the family. He was an outstanding student and loved the Lord. As he grew up he began serving in church as a Sunday School Teacher and was now happily married with a baby on the way.

However, two more children followed and developed troubling patterns; Sarah, their outgoing cheerleader, had been involved in every aspect of the church. She made excellent grades and was vice president of her high school student body. But she was out of control on the weekends; she rarely met her curfew and telltale signs left in the car revealed alcohol and sexual activity. Dropping out of college in her junior year, she had married and divorced within two years. Now with two children, she was struggling to make ends meet.

Brad was undoubtedly the most intellectual of the entire family; his siblings called him "Spock." He was always involved in some experiment and had developed an interest in Computer Science. However, his grades began to fall in his senior year. One day his mother accidentally noticed a pop-up window on his computer that was an invitation to a pornographic webpage. She looked at the history and was shocked to find that Brad was looking at hundreds of pornographic and occult websites. While Brad overcame his academic troubles, graduated from college, and was working for an IT company in San Francisco, sadly, he had "come out" a few years earlier and revealed that he had been gay since high school.

A Grim Reality for Parents and the Church

These stories are fictitious but similar ones are played out every day in the lives of many families in the American church. No doubt you are aware of hurting families in your church.

Independent research groups indicate that seventy-five to ninety percent of our young people walk away from church upon graduating from high school. Every minute we lose four youth, every hour we lose over two-hundred, every day we lose over five-thousand, and every year we lose over two-million. Our children are walking out the doors of the church never to return.[1]

Think about the enormity of losing two million children to the world every year. Something is definitely wrong.

Parents are truly blindsided here. Of the Americans who call themselves born again Christians, only about nine percent have a biblical worldview. The majority lose their virginity by their second year of college. With more than fifty percent of Christian marriages ending in divorce, the church's divorce rate is slightly worse than that of secular society.

"Parents are truly blindsided here."

Consider the "wolves" that attack families today: education that undermines Christian beliefs, bullies, peer pressure, discrimination against Christians, drugs, the homosexual agenda, sexually transmitted diseases, child abductions, sexual predators, school violence, pornography, gangs, and the occult, to name a few. This growing list seems to never end. What is a parent to do with these real threats? Is God not protecting us?

Scripture provides a warning for parents:

"Be sober, be vigilant; because your adversary the devil walks about like a roaring lion, seeking whom he may devour" (1 Peter 5:8).

The Lord Jesus gave us a warning but also added a promise in John 10:10:

"The thief does not come except to steal, and to kill, and to destroy. I have come that they may have life, and that they may have it more abundantly."

Why is the thief stealing, killing, and destroying our families? Since Jesus promises to give us abundant life, why are these wolves consuming our families? Is there a way out of this disaster for families? The answer is yes. There is a way out.

Truthfully, Jesus Himself is the answer to each one of these "wolves." In a very real way, you need something other than a "pray and cross your fingers" approach most parents adopt. The solution is amazingly simple and practical; parents need to make disciples of their children in the same manner that Jesus made disciples.

Deep Pain in Parents and Grandparents, But There is Hope!

Many of us have experienced the departure of a child or grandchild from the church. This issue is a sore subject for countless parents. The pain is real. But God can "restore what the locusts have devoured" (Joel 2:24-25). You also know "that all things work together for good to those who love God, to those who are the called according to His purpose" (Romans 8:28). May the saying from Proverbs 22:6 come true in your life: "Train up a child in the way he should go, and when he is old he will not depart from it." May you remain faithful and steadfast in praying and ministering to those who have lost their way on the path of life.

Don't lose sight of the fact that there is hope for your children and grandchildren! If you have taken them to worship, if you have had them under the preaching of the word, and if you have prayed for them, then seeds have been planted. It is no accident that you know and love the Lord and that He has placed your children under your care. Your hope is not in any parenting technique the world has to offer but in an all-powerful God who loves you and is working in your life. Take comfort in the fact that God answers prayer and that you have made sure that your children and grandchildren have heard the word of God. Some plant, some water, but God gives the increase" (1 Corinthians 3:6-7).

At the same time, in large part, you are the answer God has provided to your own prayers. As noted, you do have a job to do with your children and that job of discipling them, in one sense, does not end this side of heaven. "Keep all His statutes and His commandments which I command you, you and your son and your grandson, all the days of your life" (Deuteronomy 6:2). The command is to grandparents, parents, children, and grandchildren to observe God's law and to do so all the days of their lives. You can and should disciple your children in the manner that Jesus did even as you grow old. The job of discipling your children is a never ending task. In one sense it will become increasingly more difficult as they grow up and leave your home but in another sense it will be natural as you will have developed a discipling relationship with them that God intended. That relationship will last a lifetime.

Start early! At the same time, if your children are older, don't be discouraged. Look at who Jesus discipled. These were grown men and so much was accomplished in their lives! Don't give up. Stay involved in your children's lives. Keep praying for them, meeting their needs, ministering to them, and sharing God's word in grace to them.

Now, you might be asking yourself what it means to disciple like Jesus did. Or, you might even be saying "it doesn't matter what Jesus did. I can't do that! I can't do anything when it comes to training my children in God's word. I wouldn't know where to start or how to proceed. I've taken parenting classes and nothing seems to work." Well, don't lose heart. This book is about helping you to understand that you can disciple your children and that you can do so like Jesus did. Yes, Jesus told you to make disciples. But, think about what He said next: "I am with you always" (Matthew 28:20). The Lord Jesus is not going to tell you to do something that He won't help you with. He will be your teacher and helper even as you disciple the children He has given you. He promised not to leave you alone but to be with you through the Holy Spirit (John 14:16). He promised to give you power to be the disciple-maker He has called you to be (Acts 1:8). What could be more reassuring? What could be better than the Master Teacher coming along side of you to help you in what He wants for your children even more than you do? That's hope!

The purpose of this book is to call your attention to a simple but difficult approach to fulfilling your role in keeping your children in the faith as they reach adulthood. In so doing, you can expect to enjoy the blessings that God intended children to be. This approach is not new; it was modeled by our Lord and Savior Jesus Christ. Although the approach is not new it is rarely practiced in the American Christian culture.

This book is not an exhaustive study on the practices of Jesus Christ in His discipleship methods or otherwise. We will not examine all the skills necessary to be a good parent. We leave these things for experts more qualified than us to write about. What we are giving you are the major components of Jesus' process of discipleship with some practical application to your children.

Of course, you need to understand what has gone wrong in the church and perhaps in your personal experience. When you understand that, it will become much easier to learn what it is that Jesus did to make disciples. To that issue we now turn.

Part I

Are You Discipling
Your Children Like Jesus?

Chapter One

The Cause of our Losses

S ome businesses are committed to Total Quality Management or TQM. A tenet of TQM says that a problem in an
organization related to service or production does not usually
relate to the people per se but rather to a faulty process. So,
when problems arise, if the fruit of the process is not meeting
the satisfaction of management, the process itself is exam-
ined to determine where improvements need to be made.

If we think about the fact that almost ninety percent of
our young people walk away from the church every year, we
must consider that part of the problem is a faulty process. In
fact, it does not go too far to say that the root cause of our
losses is a faulty discipleship process that has been used by
most Christian parents for decades.

In the average Christian home the total time spent on
biblical training is less than five hours a week. With less
than five hours of biblical training a week and more than
eighty hours of non-biblical training/influence per week
from various sources, the non-biblical influence easily wins
out shortly after our children leave home. As a result, our
children and future generations are lost to the world.

"...The total time spent on biblical training is less than five hours a week."

This faulty process is based, in part, on knowledge apart from God and mere information transfer rather than the development of deep, lifetime relationships with God and man. The emphasis in secular society is on numerous but shallow relationships even within families. Consequently, there is no lasting fruit for individuals or for God's kingdom. Jesus' process was just the opposite; He developed deep relationships with His disciples and they turned the world upside down. That's the kind of fruit you want!

Now, Jesus is not anti-education. He simply understood what we must understand: "the fear of the Lord is the beginning of knowledge" (Proverbs 1:7). With regard to the faulty process, the quest for knowledge apart from God can be traced back to the original sin when Satan deceived Adam and Eve. They wanted knowledge apart from God but their sin involved so much more. They wanted to be completely independent from God. They wanted to be autonomous, that is, a law unto themselves. They apparently didn't realize the full implications of their desire and the fact that their relationship with God would be destroyed as a result of seeking that independence.

The worldly training system we have bought into (as designed by Satan) is the opposite of what Jesus Christ did in making disciples. Jesus imparted biblical knowledge and wisdom, but more importantly, He cultivated deep trust from, heart relationships with, and a lifelong commitment to His disciples.

Jesus said "For what is highly esteemed among men is an abomination in the sight of God" (Luke 16:15). The world highly esteems secular education, that is, knowledge apart from God. At the same time, virtually everything in our culture erodes deep relationships. This trap has snared many Christians.

Consider a situation in which the apostle Paul found himself. He wrote to the Corinthian church:

> For I consider that I am not at all inferior to the most eminent apostles. Even though I am untrained in speech, yet I am not in knowledge. But we have been thoroughly manifested among you in all things. Did I commit sin in humbling myself that you might be exalted, because I preached the gospel of God to you free of charge (2 Corinthians 11:5-7)?

False apostles had come into the church and were leading the people astray. One of the things these false apostles valued was the educational system of their Greek culture and the professional orators who rose from that system. They would speak in a particular rhetorical style and get paid quite well for it.

These men were drawing the Corinthians away from the truth by belittling Paul and the gospel he preached. They said he was inferior to them because he was so poor as an orator that he couldn't even charge money for his speeches. Paul defends himself by saying that he was not inferior to these skilled orators. Even though he was untrained in their ways he was not untrained in knowledge. The word he used for untrained in the Greek is *idiotes* from which we get our word idiot! The world called him an idiot. But as he said, he had true knowledge. What knowledge was he talking about? He was talking about the knowledge of God and His gospel!

The reason he did not charge to minister to them had nothing to do with his being inferior but with his being humble. He preached free of charge so as not to create a stumbling block for the gospel.

The point is that these Greeks valued the world's system of education and skill. Even many in the church strayed from the truth because of the allure of the world. The same is true in our day. You must never be tempted to buy into the world's system especially when it comes to your children. Your knowledge of the gospel and your relationship with your children is more important than any rhetorical skill, method, or information they can get from any other source. Do you want your children to be educated? Of course you do. But, discipleship is the key.

Let's take another look at the discipleship process used by Jack and Mary Johnson. Jack and Mary were busy earning a living and serving in the church. Their family had the best living conditions, experiences, and education that the world had to offer. They held high respect and esteem in the community and the church. But they were not faithful in making disciples of their children. As far as they knew, they were doing all the right things but they were so busy that they had little time left for discipleship. In some sense their children were "spiritual orphans." With their children the relationships were shallow, discipline was lacking, and protection was missing. Jack and Mary depended on the church to do what God had called them as parents to do. While the church's mission was to equip them to disciple their children, it had actually assumed their role and led Jack and Mary into thinking that was the way things were supposed to be. Without realizing it, they had all embraced a faulty process of mere information transfer and shallow relationships. The end result was that Jack and Mary along with their children were suffering for it. The children were in search of deep relationships and their busy parents were providing food, shelter, and secular education. As they entered their teen years they began to bond with their peers, with entertainment, with members of the opposite sex, with sports, and with technology in an unprotected environment.

The Fruit of Jesus versus the Fruit of the Contemporary Church

The Lord Jesus said that we will know a tree by its fruit: "Either make the tree good and its fruit good, or else make the tree bad and its fruit bad; for a tree is known by its fruit" (Matthew 12:33). Jesus is making a point about a person's heart. Whatever is in the heart comes out. If one has an evil heart then the fruit will be evil. If one has a good heart, that is, a heart transformed by Christ, the fruit will be good. We can make an application to the discipleship process. If our process is not in line with Scripture, then we cannot expect to bear the good fruit of genuine or mature disciples of Christ. If the process is biblical, then we can expect the good fruit we desire.

Upon examining the fruit of our discipleship process (two-million young people per year lost; only nine percent of Christians maintaining a biblical worldview), we can clearly see that the process itself is faulty. Using the analogy that Jesus used, the tree (faulty discipleship process) is bearing bad fruit and leading millions to apostasy.

We are not negating the role of God in the salvation of children. But, the Bible is clear that parents have a responsibility to follow Christ. From our side of the equation, the solution is really quite simple: make disciples like Jesus did! If Christian parents will begin following Jesus' model of making disciples their fruit will look much more like His fruit. And, also like Jesus, they will retain their fruit. This is your calling; you must disciple your children like Jesus.

A Lack of Emphasis on *How* Jesus Made Disciples

Much has been written about the evangelistic requirement of The Great Commission and many have rightly pointed out that the emphasis here is making disciples, not simply converts. But there is a profound dearth of teaching on the process of disciple-making as demonstrated by Jesus and the implications that His method could have on the church today. What did Jesus mean when He said "make disciples?" Considering the way He made disciples and the resulting fruit, Christ must have had something very different in mind than what the church is doing today.

There are four major components in Jesus' method of discipleship.

Jesus Told His Disciples to Follow Him While He Showed Them How to Follow God

1. Jesus Was With His Disciples and He Took Them Into the World
2. Jesus Constantly Taught Scripture and Showed His Disciples How to Minister
3. Jesus Sent His Disciples Out in Twos to Protect Them From Wolves

Let's compare Jesus' approach to training with the world's approach.

Two Training Approaches

Jesus' Training Approach	World's Training Approach
Follow me only, a trustworthy teacher	Follow many teachers of questionable values
With disciples most of the day	With disciples in spare time

Constantly teach Bible and show disciples how to minister to others (80+ hours)	Constantly teach non-biblical information, little biblical training (less than 5 hours)
Send out adult disciples in two's to protect	Send out child disciples alone

Priorities and Results of Two Approaches

Jesus' Training Approach	World's Training Approach
Goal- Make disciples: followers of Christ	Goal- Well educated student, respected job, affluence and popularity
Goal- A few deep relationships	Goal- Numerous superficial relationships
Results- Eternal impact	Results- Temporary self gratification

We'll come back to this little chart again as the heart of Jesus' disciple-making method revolved around these four dynamics.

Making Disciples: The Priority of Jesus Christ

It's been said if you want to find out what the most important thing is to an individual pay attention to his final words. In John 17 we have some of the final words of Jesus on earth as He prayed to His heavenly Father. At the heart of Jesus' prayer was His presentation of the fruit of His ministry to God: His disciples.

I have manifested Your name to the men whom You have given Me out of the world. They were Yours,

31

You gave them to Me, and they have kept Your word. Now they have known that all things which You have given Me are from You. For I have given to them the words which You have given Me; and they have received them, and have known surely that I came forth from You; and they have believed that You sent Me. I pray for them. I do not pray for the world but for those whom You have given Me, for they are Yours. And all Mine are Yours, and Yours are Mine, and I am glorified in them. Now I am no longer in the world, but these are in the world, and I come to You. Holy Father, keep through Your name those whom You have given Me, that they may be one as We are. While I was with them in the world, I kept them in Your name. Those whom You gave Me I have kept; and none of them is lost except the son of perdition, that the Scripture might be fulfilled. But now I come to You, and these things I speak in the world, that they may have My joy fulfilled in themselves. I have given them Your word; and the world has hated them because they are not of the world, just as I am not of the world. I do not pray that You should take them out of the world, but that You should keep them from the evil one. They are not of the world, just as I am not of the world (John 17:6-16).

Now, Jesus could have presented many good works that He had performed during His ministry. He could have presented to God His victories over Satan. He could have presented His command over the waves or the wind. He could have presented the fact that he fed the five-thousand. He could have presented people who had been healed, people who had demons cast out of them, or people He raised from the dead.

"Parents, God has given you your children to disciple them."

But Jesus didn't present to God any of these miracles. He presented the most important thing that the Father had given Him: His disciples. Parents, God has given you your children to disciple them.

After asking God to glorify Him, Jesus demonstrated by His prayer in John 17 that making disciples was His life's primary mission. Parents, making disciples is your primary calling and your children are your primary disciples in life. Jesus recognized that His disciples had been given to Him by God for a very short season. The same is true of you. Your children have been given to you by God for a very short season and one day you will present them to God as your primary fruit. Make sure that Jesus' priority is your priority.

Abandoning the Practices of the Founder

In 1999, my business partner and I sold a company we founded in 1983. In its eighteen year history, the business had been dedicated to the Lord and grew to one hundred thirty employees. Our business was centered on strong relationships and service to our customers. Unfortunately, the company that acquired the business abandoned that vision. They dismantled the processes and practices of the founders and they got rid of our customer service managers. Their focus was on more profit but they lost a massive amount of business. Customer relationships were gone. Within a few short years the new company had lost all the major accounts and the number of employees had fallen from one-hundred thirty to only nine.

What is happening in the church is not very different. Jesus spent three years showing us how to make disciples. He taught His disciples in the morning, when they sat, when they traveled, and when they were about to retire for the day. He personally assumed the task and He constantly performed it. He protected His disciples by sending them out in twos. He presented His most important work, the work of making disciples, to God just prior to His crucifixion. Then He commanded us to make disciples.

"Jesus knows how to make disciples better than anyone. Why would we ignore His approach?"

Like the new owners of the company mentioned above, when it comes to discipling our children, we have abandoned the practices of the founder. Jesus gave us a model to follow. He is the Lord of the universe. Jesus knows how to make disciples better than anyone. Why would we ignore His approach?

Since many parents are not following Jesus in this regard, many have lost their relationships with their children. The church is reaping the huge consequences of not following Christ in her discipleship practice. Satan knows how Jesus made disciples as described in the four components above. He has convinced Christians to give their children to him nearly all day long. Satan is using these four components to make disciples of his own out of our children. Again, Jesus said, "The thief does not come except to steal, and to kill, and to destroy. I have come that they may have life, and that they may have it more abundantly" (John 10:10). Will your children be discipled by Satan or by you? Will your children be vulnerable to destruction by the devil or will your family enter the abundant life that Jesus promised?

Chapter Two

Wall Street or Streets Paved with Gold? Investing in Your Children

Hard times hit every family sooner or later. The Dean family is no exception; my father passed away in 1999. Among other things, he was a good provider and had made sure my mother would be taken care of financially when he was gone. With my help, she took what he had left her and put it in an annuity that would provide her a monthly income and enable her to leave something when God took her home. Then something happened that had never happened before; the stock market had massive declines in successive years. Her holdings were cut in half in short order. Just when it looked like things would make a comeback, down the market went again. To add insult to injury, as you know, a major financial crisis gripped the country in late 2008. Mom no longer has a monthly income from that annuity and her investment is all but gone.

Perhaps you have had a similar experience. Everyone I know has lost something in the recent economic crisis; investments, savings, homes, or jobs. The Scripture is true; earthly wealth is not forever, riches are uncertain, and we must never put our trust in them (Proverbs 27:24; 1 Timothy

6:17). It is not wrong to make wise investments. We are told
to do so (Matthew 25:15f). We simply should not count on
them. Our trust should be in God.

Think further about this matter. While the Bible talks
about stewardship and investment, it points us to an investment of greater value than the stock market and to treasure
that is of greater value than anything the world has to offer.

I want you to think about treasure, investment, and discipleship all at the same time. But I want you to think about
it in light of the world in which your children live. In the
end, the issue that will confront us is whether or not we are
ultimately investing in Wall Street or the Streets of Gold that
are to be had in Christ.

The Influence of the World on Your Children

In 1942, C.S. Lewis published *The Screwtape Letters*,
a story in which a demon, Screwtape, gives instruction to
his demon nephew Wormwood on how to tempt human
beings and one in particular known as the Patient. Screwtape
points out that their job is to confuse people. Their temptations are not so overt but subtle. For example, he notes that
"the safest road to hell is the gradual one – the gentle slope,
soft underfoot, without sudden turnings, without milestones,
without signposts." The task is to keep a person deluded. In
the demon's words, "a moderated religion is as good for us
as no religion at all – and more amusing." He upholds the
virtue of "contented worldliness," again, a virtue from the
demon's perspective.[2]

Think about your children and worldliness here. The
world constantly exerts varying pressures upon them to
which they respond in such a way that they are constantly
conformed to it. In the face of that reality, the apostle John
gives us a sobering warning: "Do not love the world or the

things in the world. If anyone loves the world, the love of the Father is not in him" (1 John 2:15).

Not long ago, a major evangelical pastor declared: "Christianity as a set of beliefs doesn't work for me. At the same time, I acknowledge the need for ritual and celebration in my life and find fulfillment and joy in many traditional practices. I light candles and ask for the prayers of the saints...These disciplines...do not require me to believe literally in angels and the Virgin Birth."[3]

A statement like that should be understood in light of what the Bible says. This pastor talks about celebration, fulfillment, and joy. But those things in his life come from religion. He loves religion but not Christ and those are two very different things. His affections are on this world and not on Christ.

The problem is that your children can love the world in so many ways that cause them to reject not only salvation but the earthly joy and peace to be had in a vital relationship with the Lord Jesus Christ. Love for the world can be obvious or subtle and you must be very careful to help your children examine their hearts in this regard on a regular basis. How subtly they can be taken in by the deceptive illusion that the world has what they need in whatever its form!

"Your children are at war."

Your children are at war. They battle Satan, their own flesh, and the world. Note John's further words: "For all that is in the world—the lust of the flesh, the lust of the eyes, and the pride of life—is not of the Father but is of the world" (2:16). They are deceived into thinking that something is from God when it is not. Further, our culture propagates "the lust of the flesh, the lust of the eyes, and the pride of life" as good in so many ways and venues.

In his book *Everyday Talk: Talking Freely and Naturally about God with Your Children*, Jay Younts points out that the world is hostile but presents itself as wonderful source of pleasure and fulfillment. It is not what it appears to be. Satan is its ruler (under the sovereignty of God) and those who don't know Christ have no idea they are ruled by Satan. They feel as if they are directing their own lives and that they do as they please. Because of this deception, the world is attractive to them.[4]

The truth is that you must teach your children to be on guard because the enemy is aggressively out to deceive them. Satan's attacks are subtle. For example, what some consider to be benign entertainment is no such thing. Everything they see or hear comes from one of two worldviews: a Christian worldview or a non-Christian worldview. Too often Christians miss this reality.

Think of any number of television shows designed to engage children: *Dora the Explorer*; *Clifford*; *Barney; Dragon Tales*. While these programs teach some good things, they are not neutral in their worldview. They exalt goodness apart from God. Where are the parents in these shows? Are there values being taught that are unbiblical? What about the prevalence of magic in some of them? These things serve to desensitize our consciences over time. Or, consider that parents on most situation comedies are portrayed as stupid or out of touch. Husbands are depicted in the same way if not worse. Even *The Andy Griffith Show* presents lying, belittlement of others, deception, drunkenness, and other things in a positive or humorous light. The point is not that you cannot watch anything on television. Watching an episode of *Andy Griffith* can be an enjoyable experience. The point is that a worldview is being put forth in each of these shows. What worldview is being presented? Are you thinking along those lines? Are you allowing television to train your children indiscriminately?

Equally problematic is the fact that those who understand such a dynamic often feel that filling one's mind with such things has no affect upon them or that they can counteract the affect with a minimal dose of God somehow. The predominant conversation of most Christians I know centers upon the various television programs they and their children watch. Their thought is that a little bit of God-talk on Sunday and Wednesday is biblical discipleship and enough to cancel out the constant onslaught of the enemy. Sadly, they are wrong. The hearts and minds of your children are being shaped by what they take in on a regular basis. If you are not filling their minds with a biblical worldview they are by necessity being molded into the world's way of thinking.

The notion that a little bit of God-talk will stop the relentless attack of the enemy is both ignorant and arrogant and is part of Satan's deception. The battlefield on which we as Christians wage war is the mind/heart. We are constantly told to "renew our minds" as Satan, the world, and our own flesh war against our souls. If you do not see your life and the lives of your children as a battle nor understand where the battlefield is, you have lost already. Their minds are corrupted daily with the constant onslaught of ideas contrary to God. Without a constant renewal of their minds they are unable to put-off the sin that so easily entangles them and put on righteousness.

Consider a recent study cited by the Telegraph.com.uk:

Teenagers spend an average of 31 hours a week online and nearly two hours a week looking at pornography. . . They spend some three and a half hours communicating with friends on MSN, and around two hours on YouTube and in chat rooms. Just over an hour is devoted to looking up cosmetic surgery procedures such as how to enlarge breasts and get collagen implants, an hour and a half is spent on family planning and pregnancy websites and one hour 35 minutes is spent investigating diets and weight loss. One in four teenagers of the 1,000 polled said they regularly spoke to strangers online but thought it harmless. One in three admitted trying to hide what they were looking at if a parent entered the room.[5]

The fact that teenagers are spending two hours a week looking at pornography is shocking enough. But, as you take a look at the way they spend the other twenty-nine hours online combined with the fact that thirty-one hours per week is equivalent to some full-time jobs, you cannot help but be confronted with the fact that these teens are being molded relentlessly minute by minute, hour by hour, day by day, by a worldview that is diametrically opposed to Christ.

Satan's deception is propagated ruthlessly. Again, Younts points out that the world says that personal peace can be found with financial security, that sexual activity should not be restricted to marriage, and that the most important thing in life is to feel good about your self. The world says to our children that the object of faith is not important but what is important is that we simply have faith. Such a subtle nuance is more often missed than not in the minds and hearts of young people (and adults as well).

Parents, you must remember that you have a different allegiance because you are subjects of a different kingdom. God's kingdom and Satan's are opposed to one another. You are in a cosmic battle. At a personal level, that battle comes down to one of loves. What do you love: Christ or the world? Do you love the things of God or the things of the world? Remember John's words and be sober minded here. Do not be deceived.

What about your children? If you walk into your fifteen year old son's bedroom and all you see on the wall are posters of worldly things and worldly people, the tone of his claim to love Christ should ring hollow at that point. It is not that you can judge his heart. But, it is time to have a talk. What is it that he really loves? The true believer increasingly hates the things God hates and loves the things God loves. Here is yet another opportunity to saturate his mind with God's view.

Too often we reject the truth for fear of being equated with some form of legalism. There is no doubt that legalism kills and we must reject it as much as we must reject libertinism. But, it is not legalistic to say that filling one's mind with images contrary to God is not only sin but destructive. Because of our flesh, we do not have the ability to fight off the resulting influence of such a steady barrage of the mind. If you do not have that ability, neither do your children. In fact, their flesh loves such. And even if they could regularly take such a barrage unscathed, who among us is willing to say that God is ambivalent about the issue? These are the very things God hates. These are the very things that put Christ on the cross. These are the very things for which Hell exists.

So, what must you do? What if you know you are not supposed to love the world and you do not want to but you have a heart that is divided? What if you confront your child and that is his response? Scripture sets forth the solution: "Do not be conformed to this world but be transformed by the renewing of your mind" (Romans 12:2a). The sense of what Paul is saying could be better rendered: "stop being conformed to this world." Your children are constantly being conformed to this world. Paul says stop. How? "Be transformed by the renewing of your mind." In other words, don't buy into the notion that the world is where your joy is. Don't let your children do so either. The only way not to be deceived is to find your joy in Christ. That joy comes by the transforming work of the Holy Spirit as you help your children renew their minds through a constant examination of their hearts and worldview as you place those things under the microscope of Scripture.

In the end, your children won't have to wonder who they are because they will have realized that they cannot make the grade on their own and that the world's grade is not what they're after anyway. It is Christ who has made the grade for them and they will know who they are as they pursue Him by grace. They will have overcome the world in Him.

Now, how do we begin to help our children in this regard? What are the practical steps? The answer is coming. But, there are a few more biblical issues we must digest first. Remember, we're thinking about treasure, investment, and discipleship.

First Things First

What is the very best thing you can do for your children? Well, surprisingly, the answer does not begin with your children. It begins with God. Paul writes, "Whether you eat or drink, or whatever you do, do all to the glory of God" (1 Corinthians 10:31). The glory of God is ultimate, not the discipleship of your children, because Christ is ultimate, not your children. While the discipleship of your children exists in the present age, it will give way to the abiding nature of glorifying God in eternity.[6]

You may have heard this little phrase, "the chief end of man is to glorify God and enjoy Him forever." That is certainly true. The question is, "what does it mean to glorify God and enjoy Him?"

Well, to glorify something is to see its worth and excellence and then enjoy it in that worth and excellence. Several years ago I had a friend who bought a brand new shiny, red, Corvette. He then put it in his garage and never drove it! He rode around town in his pick-up truck because he didn't want to put miles on his Corvette. Now, there is a sense in which he had respect for the Corvette, but, he did not glorify it. The excellence of a Corvette is not only in its beauty but in its being driven. The only way to exalt that excellence is to drive it. That is what it means to glorify a Corvette. You enjoy it in its excellence.

Now, what is more excellent than God? To glorify, or worship God, is to give Him praise, adoration, honor, and glory for His beauty. But, it is also to live in His glory. It is to enjoy Him for at His right hand are pleasures forevermore. He is the all satisfying water that never gives out. And, if we are to do all that we do for God's glory, enjoying Him must have a practical application. That includes discipling your children because He has commanded you to. Practically speaking then, to worship God is to participate in His discipling activity as He draws others by and into His glory.

You must see the training of your children in connection to the glory of God. That is your motivation. You will find joy in this supreme activity because your heart longs to glorify God and He wants you to disciple your children for His glory. Your goal will not only be to glorify God, but to see that your children glorify God. Your goal will be that your children enjoy God. Discipling your children like Jesus is a life of supreme joy.

Treasure, Investment, & Discipleship

As noted, the stock market is always a hot topic among contemporary Americans. Aside from those who are into day or swing trading or even those who have ventured into the world of forex, the average laborer is certainly concerned with his retirement plan.

At the same time, the Scripture is also quite clear that earthly investments are not ultimate. The Lord Himself admonished the rich young ruler: "If you want to be perfect, go, sell what you have and give to the poor, and you will have treasure in heaven; and come, follow Me" (Matthew 19:21). Now, we often miss the point and focus on what Jesus wants us to give up. In fact, we often think of the burden placed upon the rich young ruler. However, the call of Christ is not a subtle form of ascetic denial. Rather, in demanding self-denial, Christ promises a far greater reward: "treasure in heaven." He promises something ultimate. Jesus is saying to the rich young ruler, "I am offering you greater treasure!"

Think about how nice it would be to have an extra five-thousand dollars lying around. You could probably use that right about now to pay off a little debt or make some needed home repairs or even put braces on your child's teeth. Or, maybe you realize you need to put a little back in savings. At the same time, there are some things you would not spend that money on. You wouldn't pay five thousand dollars for a new toaster or a new set of tires for your ten-year old car. You would hang onto that money! But, what if someone offered you a brand new car right off the show room floor for that same money? Or, what if someone offered you a brand new beach house with an ocean front view dead center of the most desired spot on the strip? You would probably part with the five-thousand dollars! You would trade that for the treasure being offered.

The real problem with us is that we don't see the reality of just how precious Christ really is. He is the treasure in the field; He is the pearl of great price; He is the living water that satisfies forever. In one sense it is difficult to part with five-thousand dollars. But, when the treasure is far greater, the decision is easy. So it is with Christ.

"The real problem with us is that we don't see the reality of just how precious Christ really is."

Moreover, it was Jesus who said,

> Do not lay up for yourselves treasures on earth, where moth and rust destroy and where thieves break in and steal; but lay up for yourselves treasures in heaven, where neither moth nor rust destroys and where thieves do not break in and steal. For where your treasure is, there your heart will be also (Matthew 6:19-21).

Note that treasure in heaven is unlike earthly treasure in that heavenly treasure is eternal. At the same time, there is a connection between treasure and heart: one's heart will be drawn to that which he considers to be treasure. Again, Christ Himself is the supreme treasure. He Himself is the treasure in heaven promised to the rich young ruler.

Now, think a little bit further with me. The things that Christ treasures are also the things that Christians should treasure and indeed do treasure as they grow in grace.

The question then arises, "What does Christ treasure?" Undoubtedly, as we alluded to earlier, He treasures His own glory above all else. He prayed to the Father, "And now, O Father, glorify Me together with Yourself, with the glory which I had with You before the world was" (John 17:5).

Further, Christ treasures His people. He treasures His disciples. He came to save them from their sin (Matthew 1:21) and He expressed His activity toward them and His desire for them in the aforementioned prayer: "And I have declared to them Your name, and will declare it, that the love with which You loved Me may be in them, and I in them" (John 17:26). Think about it; that means He treasures you! What an amazing thing!

While other treasures could be mentioned, the two already noted are actually combined by Christ again in prayer: "Father, I desire that they also whom You gave Me may be with Me where I am, that they may behold My glory which You have given Me; for You loved Me before the foundation of the world" (John 17:24). Christ treasures His disciples (you) so much that He wants them to be with Him and behold His glory. The implication is that nothing is greater to behold than His glory and He wants you to see it.

Now, if Christ treasures the reality of His disciples giving glory to Him because He treasures them and His glory, then we should treasure the same. Thus, if your heart is where your treasure is then your heart should long for Christ's disciples to behold His glory. The resulting dynamic is a commitment to a new kind of investment: an investment in your children seeing Christ in all of His glory. That translates into an investment in biblical discipleship for your children. And please, don't miss the word I'm using: investment. You are investing in treasure: real treasure.

I am arguing for a new kind of investment here. Invest time in the word and invest time in your children and you will be investing in the glory of Christ. The dividends are eternal: treasure in heaven. And, when you think along these lines, the glory of God and the joy of your children; the commit-ment to make disciples of your children in accordance with the Great Commission; and in seeking these things as the treasure they are, you will then be ready and willing to make the greatest investment for you and your family that you could ever make.

Chapter Three

Therefore Go and Make Disciples of All Your Children

Parents Obeying the Great Commission

A conversation about making disciples would never be complete without looking at the Great Commission in Matthew 28:18-20.

> And Jesus came and spoke to them, saying, "All authority has been given to Me in heaven and on earth. Go therefore and make disciples of all the nations, baptizing them in the name of the Father and of the Son and of the Holy Spirit, teaching them to observe all things that I have commanded you; and lo, I am with you always, even to the end of the age." Amen.

Jesus' command to "make disciples" is far more critical for parents when it comes to the issue of raising children than most imagine or understand. We know that Jesus spoke this mandate just before His ascension to heaven. The life and example of our Lord and Savior points to this directive;

our world has been forever changed by Christians who have obeyed Jesus in carrying out the Great Commission. But, how many of us truly understand the issue of making disciples and how many of us apply this command rightly when it comes to our children?

"Jesus showed us how to make disciples; why don't we follow His example?"

Immediately following three years of making disciples and presenting them to God, Jesus commanded us to do the same. When Jesus gave us the Great Commission what did He have in mind for us to do? He wants us to do what He did; it's really very simple. Jesus showed us how to make disciples; why don't we follow His example?

The Great Commission does not merely refer to going to foreign lands to preach Christ. In fact, the command is not even "Go" as most people suppose. The word that we translate "Go" in English is a participle in Greek (the original language in which the New Testament was written). A better translation would be "as you go." So as you are going about your business, your daily routine, and the life that God has given you in the context He has placed you, He has commanded you to do something: make disciples!

Now, each of us certainly has a responsibility to evangelize others as we go and we certainly have a responsibility to be involved some way in taking the gospel to the nations. But, parents, as you go throughout life, you are to make disciples. That life includes your home and the primary disciple-making responsibility you have been given by God is your children. To put it simply, you are to develop a lifestyle of discipleship when it comes to your children.

Let's break it down further. Jesus commands us as we are going to make disciples, which includes two dynamics: baptizing and teaching. A clear picture should form in your mind. Here go the parents. They have their disciples (children) with them. The parents are making disciples of their children as they go into their world. They baptize the children at the appropriate time. But not only are the children immersed in water at a baptism event, they are immersed daily by their parents in the Father, Son, and Holy Spirit. They are immersed daily in the Word. The parents are teaching their children to practice all the things that Christ commanded. And, if they are teaching their children to obey every command of Jesus, they are teaching and preparing their children to make disciples.

Again, many Christians misinterpret the Great Commission and the purpose of Christ. They read into it evangelism of others or missions only. They miss the point of discipleship completely. But even when Christians recognize and acknowledge the command to make disciples and apply it to their children, so often they cheapen the practice of discipleship and reduce it to an activity that happens for an hour or two per week.

The challenge of making disciples who will then be disciple-makers themselves lies in teaching the converted to obey the commands of Christ. When it comes to your children, the only difference is that you are to train them to obey Jesus whether they are converted or not.

Teaching your children to obey the commands of Christ is more than teaching doctrine. It is more than the transfer of information. This teaching involves applying doctrine to their hearts that they might obey. Obedience in the biblical sense never involves mere outward conformity to the law. Rather, obedience issues forth from a heart that has been changed. In the case of unsaved children, we are praying that God will change their hearts along the way through the discipling process.

In the church today so much of what is called evangelism and discipleship falls short of the biblical definition. In-depth discipleship is both formative (on-going) and corrective. The formative nature of discipleship is simply dealing with sin at the heart level through an ongoing lifestyle of self-examination, putting off sin, and putting on righteousness through the renewing of the mind. Obedience comes from a heart that is being sanctified. The corrective nature of discipleship is the practice of dealing with personal and interpersonal sin in a biblical fashion.

The bottom line is that your family must be transformed into a discipling community; a community that adheres to the biblical mandate of mutual edification for the building up of your children, the training of your children for the work of the ministry, and the encouragement of your children for the task of evangelism and missions. You are to make disciples of Jesus out of your children.

Discipleship as Designed by God and Practiced by Jesus

The idea behind Jesus' approach takes us back to a much earlier time. God said, "And these words which I command you today shall be in your heart. You shall teach them diligently to your children, and shall talk of them when you sit in your house, when you walk by the way, when you lie down, and when you rise up" (Deuteronomy 6:6-7). This commandment to teach diligently God's word to children was given to parents and grandparents by God through Moses just after God had provided the Ten Commandments. A promise accompanied God's command that if it was faithfully followed their days would be prolonged, life would go well, they would prosper and multiply, and they would receive a blessed land.

You can meet someone weekly for prayer and accountability but that is not making disciples like Jesus did; that is a "microwave approach." You can attend church but that is not making disciples. You can teach a class at church but that is not making disciples like Jesus did. You can preach the gospel but that is only a part of making disciples. You can win souls but that is only a small part of making disciples.

Jesus commanded all of us to make disciples and this practice was the very heart of His ministry. If you do not disciple your children, then who will? If you will not disciple your children, then they will become "spiritual orphans" and will likely become a part of the mass exodus of our young people from the church.

When it comes to discipling your children, the primary focus, as noted earlier, is the glory of God in their lives. Of course, your motivation toward your children is to do them good as well. Although no parent has the ability to measure up to our Lord and Savior Jesus Christ, every parent has the ability to make better choices to disciple like Jesus did.

Discipling Like Jesus Deals with the Main Issue: Sin

Why must we make such an emphasis on discipling our children in the sense of teaching them to obey every command of Christ? Remember that Satan is out to destroy your children; not people in general, but your children. Now, he uses a very powerful weapon against them: their own sinful nature along with its sinful desires and tendencies. Too many Christian parents fail to recognize that their young children are indeed enemies of God if they don't know Christ regardless of how well behaved they are. Your children are not spiritually neutral when they come into this world. Your children have the potential of committing any sin known to man. Of course, God's restraining grace is at work so that no one sins as much as he could. But, you must be aware of the force that drives your child before he comes to know Christ: it is sin and has affected every aspect of his being. Don't let that cherub-like appearance fool you.

Of course, you do see that sinful nature come out. Think about infants throwing temper tantrums; young children being overtly selfish; older children fighting with one another; and the trouble that teens get into so often. The reality is that sin lurks at their door constantly.

Now, what is the point? The point is that you must disciple your children biblically if their sinful nature is to be overcome by the power of the Holy Spirit. Your primary focus is not behavior modification but heart transformation. If your only focus is on the behavior of your child then you will raise up a hypocrite who is still headed for Hell. Behavior is certainly important but it's not the main issue.

"Your primary focus is not behavior modification but heart transformation."

Self-esteem is Not the Problem

Or, maybe you've bought into the notion constantly foisted upon us by the world that the most important thing you can do for your children is to enhance their self-esteem. A recent story was posted by an ABC news affiliate out of Birmingham, AL entitled "Increasing Self-Esteem, Decreasing Violence." From the story:

> More people have been killed this year than at the same time last year. And for community leaders, the numbers are alarming... A group called Cover to Cover believes the answer lies in self-esteem. So, they are reaching out to four Birmingham neighborhoods where violence often occurs. A team of adults did a few simple deeds by giving haircuts to boys and makeovers to girls while repeating three simple words. "We love you," said George W. Stewart, coordinator of Cover to Cover. The event called I

am your brothers- sisters keeper, touched nearly 100 kids and teenagers ranging in age from 5 to 18 years old. "They care and they want to give us a chance," said Shelby Wilson, an eighth grader. Wilson got the chance to be pampered and respected for a day.[7]

Is the reason we have violence really due to a lack of self-esteem? Is the answer giving kids haircuts? It all seems so simple. But, our problem, as noted, is much deeper than that. Our problem is in our nature: we are sinful to the point of violence when we are focused on self. So are your children. Focusing on self is like throwing gasoline on a fire. Such a dynamic will only serve to increase violence.

The message of self-esteem militates against a true knowledge of one's self before God and therefore militates against salvation and sanctification. The self-esteem movement can be described in no less a term than idolatrous as one worships self instead of God who alone is worthy of worship. It can also be described as deadly as one fails to see his enmity against God when he sees himself as good.

Moreover, the self-esteem movement is truly an attack on the gospel of Christ. Jeremy Lelek, President of the Association of Biblical Counselors, noted that some Christians try to tone down the message of self-esteem to a certain degree but in so doing still distort the gospel message.

Christian's have attempted to squelch the human-istic bent of this worldview by saying such things as, "Since God died for you, you are special," but in so doing they remove the glory of redemption from God's merciful and graceful character and place it upon the significance of the one receiving such mercy and grace (i.e., self). Therefore, "Jesus died for me because I'm special" usurps the gospel message of

'Jesus died for me, the undeserving, because he is an infinitely merciful and amazing God." The former diminishes a person's sense of desperation for their greatest need, God's grace, while the latter recognizes this desperation, and therefore fosters a deeper sense of gratitude for God's incomprehensible goodness.[8]

The reality is that all, including your children, are born dead in sin, haters of God, and deserving of His eternal judgment (Ephesians 2:1-3). You need to understand that they have committed spiritual adultery. But, the wonder of the gospel is that despite their sinful disposition and actions, God has set His love upon the spiritually adulterous, drawn them with chords of love, and made them His bride in Christ. That is a message that will fill one's heart with wonder and love for a merciful God. It is a message that gives hope and meaning and indeed fulfillment in life. It is the message you must constantly give your children. They need Christ and by giving them Christ you are discipling them like Christ. You are doing the best thing you can do for them.

Now, aren't your children supposed to know that you love them and indeed feel that you love them? Of course they are. You might be thinking, "Am I not supposed to create a protective home environment for my children? If I keep them away from the world's influence, won't that be the best thing I can do for them?" While that loving home with its protective atmosphere combined with your diligent watch against wolves is critical, that dynamic is not your primary focus either. Your focus is Christ.

Your Life Focused on Christ

Think about your need to provide that protective environment. We'll talk about the friends your children hang out with, the school they attend, and the various influences on their lives that need to be carefully monitored. At the same time, you must consider your own influence and its potentially negative impact upon your children if you are not focused on Christ and His command to disciple them. You must also consider their sinfulness in that context.

For example, a recent survey indicated that most adults believe that the commercialization of childhood is damaging to young people and that children feel pressured to own the latest designer clothes and computer games, among other material goods.[9] From where does that pressure come? In a general sense that pressure comes from the materialistic philosophy they are being taught by the culture, but, by their own parents as well! Parents, you must be constant and diligent in the training of your children. You must also be mindful that your pursuits will become their pursuits and that your everyday talk about money and material things will over shadow Bible study with your children if there is a contradiction. Your lifestyle in any area will overshadow your teaching if they contradict one another. Your children will get the message of how to apply the teaching of Scripture in a sinful way or they will see the message as unimportant as they look at your self-centered lives. Satan, the world, and the flesh all conspire against your children to take their hearts away from Christ. You must not give ammunition to the enemy.

It is difficult to live for God's glory in this world. The culture of the individualized self is manifest at earlier ages with each passing generation. What should be more alarming is the actuality that biblical prohibitions against selfism, materialism, greed, pride, and vanity are all but rejected even by most Christians. The notions things will make us happy, we must like what the world likes, we must have what the world has, and we must be well thought of by the world, are attitudes associated with those who don't truly know God. The fact that these attitudes should be found in children, and indeed among Christians, merely reveals the spiritual poverty in which the church finds herself today.

But, when you deal with your own heart and then demonstrate to your children that your hope is not in wealth or that your joy is not in wealth, then you will have an impact on them for their good. Certainly work, good stewardship, and wise financial planning for the future glorify God. But, in the end, can your children tell that your ultimate love lies elsewhere?

So, in that protective environment you have created for your children, are you influencing them toward Christ by faithfully discipling them like Jesus or are you inadvertently leading them away from Christ by your own everyday focus, actions, and talk?

We've engaged in laying a foundation to this point. We've even done some generalizing and hit some major points with a broad brush stroke. You must be wondering how to implement some of these things practically. You must be wondering what specifics you need to focus on in discipling your children like Jesus. Well, to those specifics we now turn.

Part II

Jesus Told His Disciples to Follow Him While He Showed Them How to Follow God.

"Imitate me, just as I also imitate Christ."
(1 Corinthians 11:1)

Chapter Four

Congratulations, You're Just the Right Person for the Job!

Why Parents Are the Best Persons for the Job

You might react like so many who discover that it is the parents' responsibility to disciple their children. "I'm not educated or trained to do this. We don't have the temperament to work with children. We don't have the gift of teaching." Over the years I have heard all kinds of excuses.

But the truth of the matter is that no one is more qualified to disciple your children than you. God uniquely designed you as your child's leader and your child as your follower. Discipling your child is like anything else in life; practice makes perfect.

> "...no one is more qualified to disciple your children than you."

There are many reasons that no one can disciple your child better than you. **First of all, there is no one who has the availability to disciple your children like you.** You have a captive audience just like Jesus had with His disciples. A part time effort will not do the job. Your local church will not do a better job than you because they only have your children a few hours per week. The schools will not disciple your children because their job is to impart knowledge, not to build relationships, and certainly not to disciple. The entertainment industry will not do it because their goal is to please the flesh; they will make disciples of the devil. Only you have the ability to be with them like Jesus was with His disciples.

Second, no one else loves your children like you do. Your fellow church members are commanded to love one another but they don't love your children like you do. School teachers do not love your children as much as you love them. The entertainment industry does not love your children at all. Only you love your children because they are your children.

Third, no one naturally knows your children better than you and your spouse. When you disciple your children, you will be the best guide to help them understand God's call on their lives. Your local church will not know your children like you. A teacher with twenty students will not know your children like you. Only you know your children like Jesus knew His disciples.

Most importantly, no one else is commanded by the Lord to disciple your children. The job of your local church is to equip the saints; to teach the saints how to disciple, how to evangelize, and how to understand the deep truths in Scripture. Furthermore, the job of the local church is to engage members in corporate worship, fellowship, and accountability. Only you have been commanded by God to disciple your children like Jesus made disciples. Only you will be held accountable by God for this task.

You Have What it Takes

Consider the ability and qualifications of the disciples. These men were average, uneducated men. We see a description of two of the most notable disciples in Acts 4:13: "Now when they saw the boldness of Peter and John, and perceived that they were uneducated and untrained men, they marveled. And they realized that they had been with Jesus." Three characteristics of Peter and John are revealed here: boldness, uneducated, and untrained. Do these characteristics sound like you? Are you bold enough to obey the Lord? Are you uneducated? Are you untrained? If you answered "yes" to those three questions then you are almost qualified. However, there is one last qualification: "And they realized that they had been with Jesus."

Parents, if you have been with Jesus, then you have the most important qualification required to disciple your children. Realizing your inadequacies and depending upon Christ is the best thing that you can do for your children. Look what these untrained and uneducated men did in Acts 17:6: "These who have turned the world upside down have come here too." May you disciple your children so that they too may turn the world upside down for Christ!

Not your Own Strength

The fact is that you cannot disciple your child in your own strength. You will need to spend time praying for your child and asking the Lord to teach you first before you teach your child. Pray Psalm 25:4-5: "Show me Your ways, O Lord; teach me Your paths. Lead me in Your truth and teach me, for You are the God of my salvation; on You I wait all the day." You will need to be diligent in reading and studying God's word yourself. "This Book of the Law shall not depart from your mouth, but you shall meditate in it day and night, that you may observe to do according to all that is written in it. For then you will make your way prosperous, and then you will have good success" (Joshua 1:8). If you will do these things, the Lord will help you and equip you to disciple your children. Be encouraged! The time you spend teaching and instructing and giving testimony to the Lord's goodness will reap rich dividends! You will never regret the time you spend with your children. Remember the words of the Psalmist: "Your word is a lamp to my feet and a light to my path" (Psalm 119:105). Allow God's word to light your path, then follow Jesus, and your children will get the best possible training!

Since Jesus did not send His disciples to be trained by teachers of questionable beliefs, neither should parents. Since Jesus was with His disciples, parents should be with their children for a significant amount of time each day. Since Jesus took His disciples out into the world for ministry, so should parents. Since Jesus was constantly teaching Scripture, glorifying God, and showing His disciples how to live, parents should do the same. Since Jesus protected His disciples, so should parents.

Change comes about in degrees; over time some parents have been convicted by the Lord to make significant life changes in order to disciple their children like Jesus made disciples. Some parents have given up their entertainment, hobbies, careers, or status. Others have changed jobs, started businesses, or sold homes and other possessions. Some have cut back on television in order to spend more time with their children. The important point is to start somewhere and to be intentional. As you assume personal responsibility for the training of your children and die to self in following the example of Jesus, then the fruit that follows will be similar to the fruit that Jesus produced.

Excuses, Objections, Fears

We mentioned some of the excuses, objections, or fears that grip parents when confronted with the notion that it is they who must disciple their children. Let's expand on a few of those and answer them.

"I am untrained; how can I disciple my child?" The answer to that question is this: no trained professional can disciple your child better than you. If you love your child and are committed to trust the Lord to help you, you have what it takes. This may sound like an oversimplification but all you really need is a Bible and prayer. James 1:5 informs us, "If any of you lacks wisdom, let him ask of God, who gives to all liberally and without reproach, and it will be given to him." The Lord says, "I will instruct you and teach you in the way you should go; I will guide you with My eye" (Psalm 32:8).

"I must work to support my family. How can I spend more time with my children?" As we mentioned earlier, no parent can measure up to the example that Jesus Christ set; we all fall short. Each family will need to prayerfully determine the options and possible sacrifices necessary to disciple more like Jesus. There are many things that can be done within the context of every family lifestyle. One thing that virtually every family can do is to simply follow Deuteronomy 6 which commands parents to teach about God when we arise in the morning, when we are sitting in our house, when we are traveling, and when we lie down at night.

God might even stretch you here. You might be able to take your children to work. Or, you might be able to work at home. Your wife might be able to come home. Some entrepreneurial families may be able to start their own family business. The possibilities are endless! Regardless of your situation, ask the Lord to help you "think outside the box" for ideas to disciple like Jesus.

"As Christian parents, we are not satisfied with losing almost 90% of our children."

"What about me? I turned out OK without this discipleship like Jesus." Praise the Lord! You are a "Daniel," who by God's grace remained faithful to His Lord despite being removed from his home to a foreign land where he was trained by pagans. He, like you, is an exception to the rule. You are part of the twelve percent who stayed in the church or returned after college. We know that the Lord will always preserve a remnant of His people. We have a few examples in Scripture about men such as Daniel and Moses who received secular training as children and teenagers yet were able to stand firm in their faith. But of course in each example, their parents were forced to let go of their children; they did not volunteer to do so. Furthermore, not every child is a "Daniel." More importantly, as Christian parents, we are not satisfied with losing almost ninety percent of our children.

Parents are Shepherds of their Children

We have all heard the analogies comparing sheep to people. The shepherd's primary job is to feed, nurture, care for, and protect his flock. The role of the shepherd is so beautifully described in the 23rd Psalm.

> The Lord is my shepherd; I shall not want. He makes me to lie down in green pastures; He leads me beside the still waters. He restores my soul; He leads me in the paths of righteousness For His name's sake. Yea, though I walk through the valley of the shadow of

death, I will fear no evil; for You are with me; Your rod and Your staff, they comfort me. You prepare a table before me in the presence of my enemies; You anoint my head with oil; My cup runs over. Surely goodness and mercy shall follow me All the days of my life; And I will dwell in the house of the Lord Forever.

As a shepherd, Jesus made sure that His disciples had all they needed; food, protection, teaching, and nurture. He led them into the world but they frequently retreated to areas of solitude where they could be refreshed. Jesus delivered the words of life to His disciples and showed them what true righteous living was all about. They traveled through perilous situations but Jesus the shepherd was with His flock so that they needed not fear. Jesus protected with His presence, His verbal discipline to His flock, and His verbal blows to the Pharisee wolves. As a result of the ministry of Jesus to His flock, they experienced eternal life and delivered that gift to countless others.

This Psalm is a wonderful guide for parents. Like Jesus, you are to provide for the needs of your children. Most of us do a great job of providing adequate food, clothing, shelter, and protection. But do you provide the protection, teaching, and nurture required of a faithful shepherd? Do you personally take your children out into the world and show them how to live the Christian life? Do you lead them to places of solitude from a dangerous and busy world? Do you personally deliver the words of life to your children? Do you teach them to be righteous? Do you walk with your children when danger is present or are they out alone and unprotected in certain situations? Do you comfort your children with discipline and use your adult stature and wisdom to ward off the wolves that they encounter? Do you provide understanding, discernment, and wisdom to your children in the presence of those who might want to destroy them?

Begin Early with your Children

Many parents are blindsided by issues and strife when their children enter their teen years. They ask the question, "Who is this person that lives in my house?" Children suddenly begin to act different, to dress different, to argue, and to withdraw from family activities. They want to do everything the culture does. Arguments ensue over appearance, curfews, and grades in school. The parents quickly lose control. Every interaction with their child becomes a war and the parents are not winning. The teen's logic makes no sense. They want to stay away from the family as much as possible. They would much rather be with their youth group and friends at school. Soon every interaction becomes so painful that the parent soon joins the youth in wanting separation. Parents can't wait to get this stranger out of their home so they begin to count the days until the teen can be sent off to college.

There is still hope for parents to restore order in the home at this point but it will be a very difficult job indeed. Starting to disciple like Jesus early is the key to avoid this heartache.

Most young parents really don't know what to do when it comes to discipleship. Looking back, we Melton's did not start early enough; if I had to do it all over again, we would have started when our kids were still in the womb. Jen was nine and Ryan was six and they had received a good amount of involvement in their lives from Donna and me. Donna quit work before they were born. I had my business under control to the point that I could be home fairly early and could get off work whenever a family or school event required my attendance. We prayed before meals and I shared my testimonies with my children. We talked some about Jesus and the gospel and had the opportunity to lead Ryan to the Lord while Jen made a profession of faith at church. We had decided before they were born that they would be raised in the church, would attend Christian schools, and would have only Christian friends. But there was nothing intentional about our discipleship for the first nine years of our parenting experience.

Wise parents begin to pray for their children while they are still in the womb. They talk to their baby about Jesus and His goodness. They read Scripture to them. Read God's word to your children early; let it begin working in their lives while they are still babies. Begin discipleship early and you will enjoy the fruit of your labors when your children enter their teens.

> "Read God's word to your children early; let it begin working in their lives while they are still babies."

Set a Godly Example for Your Children to Follow

The apostle Paul wrote: "Imitate me, just as I also imitate Christ" (1 Corinthians 11:1). There are special times in your child's life that he or she wants to be like you. You are for a season his role model and his example to follow. He walks like you, talks like you, and wears the same clothes as you. I remember my son Ryan carrying one of my old briefcases pretending to talk with business associates on one of my expired cell phones and playing with a hand-me-down PDA.

I remember my daughter Jen emulating my wife Donna; playing house and baking pretend foods for me. I remember her playing with dolls; caring for them, feeding them, reading to them, changing their diapers, picking them up, and caressing them when they cried. Your children pick up the character traits and habits of the people they are around.

Jesus' desire was to walk in total communion and obedience to His heavenly Father. He knew that He was going to be our example for living the life that pleases God. Jesus pointed out that He Himself did what His Father did.

> Then Jesus answered and said to them, "Most assuredly, I say to you, the Son can do nothing of Himself, but what He sees the Father do; for whatever He does, the Son also does in like manner. For the Father loves the Son, and shows Him all things that He Himself does; and He will show Him greater works than these, that you may marvel" (John 5:19-20).

As parents, you have the unique and wonderful privilege to closely emulate your Lord Jesus and thereby in some sense shape your child into His image. You can walk in close fellowship with the Lord and His word and then do as Jesus did.

Arresting Thoughts on Sending your Children to Others

Jesus called His disciples to follow Him and Him alone. He said, "Follow Me, and I will make you fishers of men" (Matthew 4:19). Now pay attention here! He *did not* tell His followers to follow other teachers. He certainly did not tell His followers to follow teachers who were unbelievers. Nor did Jesus tell his disciples to follow teachers who were of questionable values. Jesus told His disciples to follow Him while He showed them how to follow God. He personally assumed the responsibility and set about the task of training His disciples.

Imagine what might have been the result if Jesus had decided to send His disciples to be trained by the secular thinkers of the day for forty hours per week. Then consider the possibilities if Jesus had sent them to the Romans for athletic training. What if Jesus and His disciples had attended all the local performances and all the gladiator events? What if Jesus had counted on the Jewish Synagogues to train His disciples once or twice per week?

The likely result would be that His disciples would have been poorly prepared for ministry and most would have left the faith. Does this sound familiar? Why would we expect our children to turn out any better?

Now contrast the approach of Jesus with the approach that many Christian parents use today. Parents don't tell their children to follow them. They instead send their children to follow all kinds of other teachers and influences; influences that often indoctrinate them into a non-biblical worldview. The fact is that your children will become like their teacher(s). Jesus said, "A disciple is not above his teacher, but everyone who is perfectly trained will be like his teacher" (Luke 6:40).

Consider the Risks of Sending Your Children to Others

Hillary Clinton authored the book entitled *It Takes a Village*.[10] One of the central ideas of the book is that in order to raise a child many teachers will be necessary. This is a popular idea in our society and unfortunately has become popular in many churches.

I am thankful for Christian teachers and coaches who are evangelizing and making disciples of children that have parents who will not assume this very important task. It is a very difficult and high calling to pour out their lives by making disciples, and to the best of their ability, by following Christ in the way that He made disciples. Praise the Lord for godly teachers and coaches as they reach the lost and "spiritual orphans!"

But consider some of the risks involved with sending your children to others for training. It may be that God wants to stretch you a bit further and give you the blessing of spending far more time with your children both for His glory, their good, and your joy. And remember, when it comes to discipling your children, you are the best person for the job.

Chapter Five

Follow the Leader: You!

Leading By Example

Today's world can be characterized by the professionalization and specialization of virtually every area of life. There are business consultants, certified mechanics, licensed plumbers, doctors of all kinds, and the list goes on seemingly forever.

This professionalization and specialization has reached the church as well. We now have "pastors" for every area one can think of including the Senior Pastor, the Associate Pastor, right on down to the singles, senior adults, college, youth, and children's pastors. There are now media, music, outreach, administrative, visitation, and even recreation pastors.

The result of this professionalization and specialization is that we are trained to depend upon others for virtually every area of our lives. This can be a good thing. We all have different gifts in the body of Christ. We should use those gifts for the glory of God. Other than using drain cleaner, I have no business trying to fix the kitchen sink, for God knows that not only will I cause more problems, I will end up spending more money and time trying to fix the drain.

However, there is at least one area that you should _never_ delegate to others. That is the discipleship of your family. The most important thing in your life after your relationship to God is your relationship with your family. You are given your children for a very short time to love, to call, to teach, to train, and to empower as they become young adults. That's exactly what Jesus did; He loved, He called, He taught, He trained, and He empowered His disciples. In so doing, He led by example.

There is something powerful that happens when we lead by example. We tell our children to "follow me." We suddenly realize that all eyes are upon us. Our family is dependent upon us to lead, to teach, and to show everyone how to live. We better get our act together and fast! We better start "walking the talk" because our family knows us better than anyone. Our family knows our faults and as we teach through the Bible the truth of our lives becomes illuminated for all to see. We have to admit and confess our sins and our transparency is an example for the rest of the family to follow. Our quiet time becomes much more focused because we know that we will be teaching our family later on in the day. We become so much more dependent on the Lord because we realize how deficient we are in our own abilities.

"There is something powerful that happens when we lead by example"

When we assume the role of leadership in our homes, something else happens. We realize that we are accountable to God for our families and we are also accountable to be better examples. God begins to work in that context. I can fool my work associates about many of my personal shortcomings. I can fool my weekly accountability partner about areas where I am not exhibiting the fruit of the Spirit in my life. My friends at church on Sunday will see me at my best.

But my family really knows me; my flaws, faults, and sins are clear to them. Our hypocrisy comes under the micro-scope and our life begins to line up with the word of God and He makes us better able to model Christ!

Rather than WWJD, What *Did* Jesus Do?

A popular saying in Christian circles is "What Would Jesus Do?" We have seen this question and its abbreviation "WWJD?" on bumper stickers, bracelets, in books, and on videos. In 1896 Charles Sheldon wrote a book entitled *In His Steps* in which he points the reader towards following the example of Christ.[11] The book and the idea of actually following Jesus made a comeback again in the 1990's; people again were measuring their actions against the hypothetical actions that Jesus would likely take.

But an even more relevant question for Christians is not a hypothetical one. The more important question is, "What *Did* Jesus Do?" After all, Jesus commanded Christians to follow Him! No less than six times in the book of Matthew did Jesus command His disciples and us to follow Him. He said "Follow Me, and I will make you fishers of men" (Matthew 4:19). "Follow Me, and let the dead bury their own dead" (Matthew 8:22). To Matthew the tax collector Jesus simply said, "Follow Me" (Matthew 9:9). We read in Matthew 10:38 the convicting words, "And he who does not take his cross and follow after Me is not worthy of Me." Jesus made a similar statement in Matthew 16:24 "If anyone desires to come after Me, let him deny himself, and take up his cross, and follow Me." Finally, Jesus said to the rich young ruler, "If you want to be perfect, go, sell what you have and give to the poor, and you will have treasure in heaven; and come, follow Me" (Matthew 19:21).

And if Jesus commanding us six times were not enough, we have some more examples in the book of John. Jesus said "My sheep hear My voice, and I know them, and they follow Me" (John 10:27). "If anyone serves Me, let him follow Me; and where I am, there My servant will be also. If anyone serves Me, him My Father will honor" (John 12:26). And then in John 21:19, "This He spoke, signifying by what death He would glorify God. And when He had spoken this, He said to him, 'Follow Me.'"

Doing what Jesus did is very hard! Jesus promised us that following Him would include sacrifice. Again, He told the rich young ruler "One thing you lack: Go your way, sell whatever you have and give to the poor, and you will have treasure in heaven; and come, take up the cross, and follow Me" (Mark 10:21). And, although as parents we are motivated by love for our children and for our desire to see them in heaven, our love for them should pale in comparison to our love for God. Jesus told us this:

> He who loves father or mother more than Me is not worthy of Me. And he who loves son or daughter more than Me is not worthy of Me. And he who does not take his cross and follow after Me is not worthy of Me. He who finds his life will lose it, and he who loses his life for My sake will find it (Matthew 10:37-39).

As parents you are commanded to love the Lord more than you love your children. Following Jesus Christ in the way you make disciples flows primarily from your love for Jesus and secondly from your love for them.

Initiative, Inquisitive, and Involved

As a parent, you are a leader of your family. John MacArthur wrote about some of the important skills of leaders in *The Book on Leadership*. He focused on the leadership skills of Jesus. MacArthur indicates that when it comes to our followers, we need the skills of taking initiative with them, being inquisitive with them, and of being involved with their lives.[12]

Taking initiative with your children can begin before they are born and should continue for their entire lives. Unfortunately, we have a tendency to do what we have experienced. If our parents were not directly involved in our training then we are not likely to be involved with our children. As we look back to the "Builder" generation (those born before 1945), the status quo was to allow schools and churches to train children. Builders were busy working to earn a living and in many households both parents worked. Sadly, many Christians today are following the same model without much thought. We must take the initiative with our children. It is hard work but the dividends are rich.

The danger of *our* generation is that we are used to being entertained and entertainment often competes with us doing the hard work of making disciples. God's word tells us, "The hand of the diligent will rule, but the lazy man will be put to forced labor" (Proverbs 12:24). This Scripture not only shows the rewards of diligence but it uncovers the fruit of laziness. Taking the initiative with your children's training will put you in charge and will bring the sweet fruit of obedience and godliness. Not taking the initiative will eventually *force* you to work; you will be busy in battle with your disobedient children and you will work the rest of your lives trying to get them back into the church when they depart.

When you are inquisitive with your children you can help them to process the knowledge that they possess. Jesus constantly asked questions of people around Him. This questioning is one of the most effective ways to help a child develop a biblical worldview. Through asking questions you can determine what he believes and doesn't believe; what he understands and doesn't understand. Proverbs 20:5 says,

"Counsel in the heart of man is like deep water, but a man of understanding will draw it out."

You are required by the Lord to teach your children but the practice of listening is just as important. As you gain understanding of each child's unique gifts and abilities you can help to guide your children in their calling. This practice is especially important with children who are not as verbally expressive as others. If you too are not conversational by nature you will miss many opportunities for discipling if you do not initiate dialog. For example, you might ask your child what his dreams are and then listen. You will learn where his heart is and you will then have an occasion to engage in a rich and fruitful exchange.

Being involved in our children's lives provides incredible opportunities to model to them how we want them to live. Jesus was with His disciples all day long and during this time He was showing them how to live the Christian life. He was ministering, praying, and engaging others in the community and all the while His disciples were there with Him observing how He lived. Proverbs 23:26 says this: "My son, give me your heart, and let your eyes observe my ways." Like Jesus, you can keep the hearts of your children by being their closest confidants and their examples of Christian love. You can show them how to pray as you encounter others with needs. You can show them how to minister as you meet the needs of others. You can show them how to witness as you talk to others about the love of Christ.

Fathers and Spiritual Leadership

The culture war rages on many fronts and affects our families in untold ways. Consider the defection of men from the battle. In a recent Barna Research study, mothers reportedly outpaced fathers in terms of spiritual activity and commitment.[13]

The study stated,

> Men may enjoy advantages in physical strength, but they are much less likely than women to exercise their spiritual muscles. This gender gap extends to the typical family unit: mothers outpace fathers in terms of spiritual activity and commitment. In fact, the Barna survey examined 12 different elements of faith behavior and perspective. Mothers were distinct from fathers on 11 of the 12 factors.

Further,

> when it comes to spiritual perspectives, a majority of mothers said they have been greatly transformed by their faith, while less than half of fathers had shared this experience. Also, three-quarters of moms said their faith is very important in their life, while this view was true among just two-thirds of fathers. Mothers were also more likely than fathers to be born again Christians, to say they are absolutely committed to Christianity, and to embrace a personal responsibility to share their faith in Jesus Christ with others.

In addition,

> Moms are also more religiously active. In a typical week, mothers are more likely than are fathers to attend church, pray, read the Bible, participate in a small group, attend Sunday school, and volunteer some of their time to help a non-profit organization. The only faith-related activity in which fathers are just as likely as mothers to engage is volunteering to help at a church.

What should we make of this development?

First, we can praise God for women who are committed to Christ. Without them, far more of our children would not be won to Christ, the current level of Christian influence in the culture would be diminished, and the future would be bleaker than it is. A home that has a woman committed to Christ is certainly more enriched for it and for that we can be grateful. And, mothers must indeed disciple their children like Jesus.

Second, at the same time, with the defection of men, a commitment to Christ will increasingly be seen as something for women and children alone. Obvious consequences regarding the loss of more men and boys as they grow to be men will ensue.

Third, this area is of special import for us here. Spiritual leadership in the home suffers when men do not take the lead. Children are not parented properly as fathers are not involved or are involved in the wrong way, male spiritual leadership is not modeled, and the upshot is a spiritually dysfunctional home. Children grow up with no experiential understanding of a biblically ordered home not only in terms of the respective roles of fathers and mothers, but also in terms of family devotions, family commitment to the church, and family commitment to gospel advance. This lack will multiply exponentially as these children form homes of their own in adulthood. You can see the ripple effects are devastating.

"Fathers must do something."

Fathers must do something. You must be the leaders God has designed you to be in the church, in your home, and in the culture at large. Your wives and children will be better for it, the church will be better for it, and the culture will benefit from it. You must engage. And, the best place to start is with your own children. Nothing less than their souls are at stake.

What about Single Moms?

You single moms may be feeling a little overwhelmed at this point. You are likely working full time and you are wondering how you can disciple your children like Jesus on top of that necessity, taking care of the household, and all the other responsibilities that come with the territory. Keep in mind that you can follow the spirit of Deuteronomy 6 by talking about the goodness of the Lord and praying with your children when you take them to school or other places; by reading Scripture (or listening to the Bible on CD) while you do the household chores; by singing hymns and praying with them when they go to bed; or by playing God-glorifying music in the mornings. There are so many ways to fill their minds with the things of God. You must simply be intentional about discipling them and trust the Lord who has you where you are for a very specific reason.

If your children must attend public school for financial reasons, talk with them daily about what they are learning. Address any misinformation that they are receiving. Teach your children in advance about the kinds of teachings that don't agree with God's word so that they will not be seduced by teachings of the world. We'll cover a number of those things a little later. As you establish the habit of focusing on the Lord when you are with your children, you will become more creative in finding ways to communicate His goodness. You will be their spiritual leader.

Part III

Jesus Was With His Disciples and He Took Them Into the World

"Then He appointed twelve, that they might be with Him and that He might send them out to preach."
(Mark 3:14)

Chapter Six

Counting the Cost: Being With Your Children

Melton Journey into Discipling Like Jesus

In the Spring of 2001, my daughter Jennifer came home from her Christian school and asked us to home school her. The leaders of her school were increasingly changing their focus from Christ to academics. The leadership had recently communicated their vision to become a "college preparatory school;" they wanted to compete with the most prestigious secular school in our community. The administration had stepped up the curriculum to an almost unbearable pace. Many of the children and many of Jennifer's friends were making a mass exodus; a few families had decided to home school. After considering the prospects of homeschooling I thought to myself, "Sure, in a hundred years," but I told her that we would pray about it.

My wife Donna had been concerned with issues related to school for some time. Our son's kindergarten classmates were watching R-rated movies. Jennifer was being attracted to the culture; she wanted to dress, talk like, and be with her peers constantly. We prayed and began to search for information so that we could make an informed decision. The Lord convicted my heart. He holds parents responsible for the spiritual training of their children. Immediately I began to teach Scripture to my children as part of their school day. Over time we made many changes to our lifestyle in order to better disciple our children. Most of the changes were a result of reading Scripture and the Lord turning my heart to my children. God's Holy word began to do His work in all our lives.

Counting the Costs of Making Disciples Like Jesus

How serious are you about following Jesus? How serious are you about discipling your children? Jesus is the One who told us to count the cost. As mentioned before, change comes in degrees. The process of sanctification begins at salvation but continues for the rest of our lives. Christ reveals more and more of Himself as we follow Him more closely. As we begin to obey His commands, we tap into the abundant life that He promised. We tap into the living vine. Jesus said,

I am the true vine, and My Father is the vinedresser. Every branch in Me that does not bear fruit He takes away; and every branch that bears fruit He prunes, that it may bear more fruit. You are already clean because of the word which I have spoken to you. Abide in Me, and I in you. As the branch cannot bear fruit of itself, unless it abides in the vine, neither can you, unless you abide in Me. I am the vine, you are the branches. He who abides in Me, and I in him, bears much fruit; for without Me you can do nothing. If anyone does not abide in Me, he is cast out as a branch and is withered; and they gather them and throw them into the fire, and they are burned. If you abide in Me, and My words abide in you, you will ask what you desire, and it shall be done for you. By this My Father is glorified, that you bear much fruit; so you will be My disciples (John 15:1-8).

Once we have tasted of the goodness of the Lord, we will return again and again for more and more of His word. We will "sell out" to the Lord.

For the parent who is truly "sold out" to Jesus Christ, it will cost everything. Look what Jesus said:

If anyone comes to Me and does not hate his father and mother, wife and children, brothers and sisters, yes, and his own life also, he cannot be My disciple. And whoever does not bear his cross and come after Me cannot be My disciple. For which of you, intending to build a tower, does not sit down first and count the cost, whether he has enough to finish it (Luke 14:26-28).

Does Jesus really want us to hate our family members? Of course not! But, He must hold the place of preeminence in your life, so much so, that the importance of your family pales in comparison. "So likewise, whoever of you does not forsake all that he has cannot be My disciple" (Luke. 14:33).

Parents, if you really want to disciple like Jesus, you will forsake all. Following Jesus Christ in the way that He made disciples will cause you to personally assume the task of making disciples; this is hard work. It will cause you to repent often for failing to "walk the talk" and show you how inadequate you are without God's help. Following Jesus will cause you to ask for forgiveness of your family often as your actions are not biblical. It will cause you discomfort as you reject some choices that most other parents are making. It will cause you to critically evaluate and give up some activities that you now enjoy. It will cost you a great amount of personal time. Discipling your children like Jesus may cause you to give up some hobbies that take time away from your family; may cause you to quit your job or change it so that you can be with your children; may cause you to lose your status in the community as you quit or change your job; or it may cause you to sell possessions such as cars, homes, boats, etc. so that you can make disciples. Following Jesus this way may leave you with less in the bank; place you at odds with extended family that will encourage you to keep the status quo; or cause you to stand out since you will be together as a family. It will place your family under scrutiny since you will be doing things differently. It will also cause you to be vigilant in protecting your family and that will lead to inconvenience.

Deny Yourself, Take Up Your Cross

Jesus told us that in order to follow Him, we will need to "deny ourselves" (Matthew 16:24). The making of a disciple is no small thing. Jesus did not live a luxurious life. He was not popular. As far as we know, Jesus didn't have any hobbies. He didn't look for shortcuts. He was willing to sacrifice His will, His time, His personal comforts, His possessions, and even His life for you and for me.

Anyone can take small steps towards making disciples like Jesus did. Any Christian parent who takes seriously the command of Jesus to make disciples can immediately begin to implement these principles into their family lives. But making disciples like Christ will require some level of sacrifice on the part of a parent.

Ultimately, committed Christian parents will examine every area of their lives to determine if what they are doing is conforming their children to the image of Christ. You may need to completely reengineer your lives.

Education vs. Discipleship

Be with your children. That's the goal. Your goal to be with your children like Jesus was with His disciples will impact the way you evaluate the way your children will be educated. One of the blessings of living in our day is the amount of educational options before us. We have the ability to send our children to public schools, Christian schools, other parochial schools, or to home school them. There are even hybrids within these broader categories; public schools offer special education for gifted students and for learning disabled students. Public schools are also now offering home school curriculums. In the home school arena, there are cooperatives and there are home school students who engage in public school sports.

Making sure that your children can read well, write well, and do math well is important and a child's calling in life may necessitate additional specialized education. But the importance of education pales in comparison to making disciples of your children. No matter what educational option you choose, that option must be an integral part of the discipling process.

> "No matter what educational option you choose, that option must be an integral part of the discipling process."

That means that your child will be involved in your life and you will be involved in his life. Dads and moms will train their children everywhere they go; at home, at work, at the park, at the grocery store, while ministering to neighbors, and while at church. Parents will be speaking about Scripture, about the goodness of the Lord, and about the way to treat others. Academics will of course be incorporated into your children's lives. Children will be learning how to work and how to serve the Lord. If you decide that the calling on your child's life necessitates training that you cannot personally provide, you should be involved in every aspect of your child's interaction with that training.

When you begin to pray about how you will disciple your child, think about which method will best fit your family situation and will best glorify the Lord. As we discussed before, no matter what method you use, you can do better to disciple like Jesus. A public school parent can literally and practically teach Scripture to her children when they arise, when they sit in the home, when they travel, and when they lie down at night.

Which method will you choose? God will guide you because He wants to help you make disciples. He will help you find creative ways to be with your child more. It really doesn't matter where you begin. The point is to start somewhere and pray that the Lord will allow you to do more and more over time to disciple like Jesus. Change doesn't usually happen all at once; it normally comes about a little at a time. As you make a commitment to follow Jesus in the area of discipleship the Lord will give you other ideas and opportunities to do more.

This is not about Homeschooling – It is about Discipleship

Some consider homeschooling the best and only choice. However, homeschooling in and of itself is not discipleship. For many families, home schooling is simply a different place to get an education. Many home schooling parents do exactly what the secular schools do; they transfer information from books to children. The goal of many Christian families is education, not discipleship. You can disciple your children like Jesus, as noted, in any number of educational contexts including home school or public school. You can fail to disciple your children in either of those contexts as well.

Homeschooling did give us the opportunity to begin the process of discipleship with our children. But, and here is the real issue, I have learned that discipleship should occur no matter where you are. The Great Commission commands us to "go into all the world and make disciples."

> "...every parent, regardless of the method they choose to educate their child, can do better to disciple their children like Jesus made disciples."

Now, many will point to the fact that most children home schooled by Christians remain in the faith. Researcher Dr. Brian Ray found that ninety-four percent of home schooled adults responding to his survey strongly agreed with the statement, "My religious beliefs are basically the same as those of my parents" and ninety-three percent continue to attend church. As noted, various ministries have found that a shocking seventy-five to ninety percent of Christian children sent to public school drop out of church and do not hold a Christian worldview after high school graduation (Homeschoolers Grown Up: What do the Facts Show? - 2004)."[14]

But, is the issue homeschooling? The answer is not really. The difference in the results between homeschooling and public schooling relates to the fact that to some degree home schooling follows the four components that Jesus practiced; parents are personally assuming responsibility for the teaching of their children, parents are with their children all day long, some parents are using Deuteronomy 6 as their training process, and the children being in the home provides protection. Keep in mind though that we are not looking at mere statistics nor are we looking at a method that simply produces good results without really going to the Scriptures for God's perspective on the subject. I repeat; the issue is not home school. The issue is discipleship.

Now, discipling like Jesus does involve being with those you are discipling. The key here is not to focus on the method but on the discipleship process. Do you need to think about making a way for your children to be with you more? Sure. Must you have a class room at home that looks like the one at school and keep a schedule like they do at school? No. Is there anything wrong with that approach? Not if you are discipling your children in the process. Again, that discipleship process will involve telling your children to follow you as you follow Christ; spending time with them and taking them into the world; teaching them Scripture and showing them how to minister; and protecting them from wolves as you prepare to send them out. Will education be part of that process? Of course it will! A prepared disciple has to interact in and with this world. But the focus will be Christ and kingdom citizenship.

But think a little further as to how to spend more time with your children. If it were possible, would it be okay to let your children study in your office with you while you work? Would it be okay for them to do so at home while Mom fulfilled her responsibilities? What about video-school? What about doing work in the car? What about dialog around academic themes from a Christian worldview perspective while you're running errands, eating dinner, or traveling?

Again, the real issue is pointing them to Christ regardless of the context. And, having your children with you provides the best context for ongoing discipleship as you keep in mind that discipleship must be the focus regardless of the educational model you choose.

Some actually have the opportunity to bring their children home or apprentice them or take them to work but are afraid to do so for any number of reasons. You may be one of those persons. That's okay. Yet, God often nudges us out of our comfort zones for His glory and our good. Let's examine those reasons and offer some response.

Encouraging Answers

"**My children need to be properly socialized.**" There is no doubt that our children need positive socialization. This is precisely why they don't need to be placed with a group of other children their age! Doing so hinders the child's ability to socialize in a setting in which they will constantly find themselves in the future: with people of all ages. When parents choose settings for training that are inclusive of people of all ages, and there are many, children learn how to relate in settings that better reflect life in the real world while being instructed by the watchful parent. By training our children to communicate and interact with people who are older and younger, they learn important lessons from the wise while learning how to care for and love the young.

"**I don't have the ability/education to teach my children.**" While this objection seems logical, it is a fallacy. There is no way a trained teacher with twenty-five children can be as effective as an untrained but loving parent with a few children. The parent knows the child; the institutional teacher does not. The parent can address issues of the child's heart; the trained educator cannot. The parent can administer one-on-one tutoring. The parent can slow down or speed up the process to meet the child's needs whereas the child may be left behind or be bored while the public school uses the "cookie cutter" approach in an attempt to teach the large class. And, one of the best byproducts of schooling your children is the joy of relearning along with them!

"**I want my children to have the same experiences that I did.**" Just a few decades ago the number one problem in school was chewing gum in class. Today the problems are rape, murder, drugs, and pregnancy to name a few. Unfortunately, we read every day about some news of violence in schools. The experiences children have today are vastly different than the experiences we had. Of course, many of the experiences we had in school are not the kind we want for our children; we want better! Paul admonishes us in Romans 12:2: "And do not be conformed to this world, but be transformed by the renewing of your mind, that you may prove what is that good and acceptable and perfect will of God."

"If I was with my children all day I would go insane." Although Scripture tells us that our children are blessings many Christian parents don't feel this way. Although this complex problem can't be adequately addressed in one paragraph, a solution is possible. It involves both parents working together to disciple their children, build stronger relationships through more family time, and remove negative influences that work against the family. Although this is hard work, enjoying your children is worth it! Moreover, "A wise son makes a glad father, but a foolish son is the grief of his mother" (Proverbs 15:20).

"We can't afford for my wife to quit her job." This may be a legitimate reason for a two income family where the income of each wage earner is below poverty level. However, a question must be asked: "Would God help us to live if we step out in faith to obey Him?" Obeying God's word regarding the training of your children is sure to bring blessings. The blessings may not necessarily come in terms of financial wealth. But with sound planning, virtually any family in America can create a lifestyle that is sustained by a one-wage earner. One of the blessings will be family memories that money cannot buy! "Trust in the Lord, and do good; dwell in the land, and feed on His faithfulness" (Psalm 37:3).

"We are in a great school district; the teachers are Christians." This may be true, but schools, like individuals must conform to the laws. Today it is unlawful for schools to teach your children the things that you value the most and it is a requirement for the schools to teach your children what you consider to be harmful to their spiritual wellbeing. Christian teachers are required by law to deny their faith in some areas as they teach.

"Most of the other children in my church go to school." This is the primary reason that ninety percent of all children who have not been discipled are leaving the church never to return. Why not let your child play Russian roulette? The odds of winning that dangerous game are eighty-three percent. The odds of winning without discipling your children are between ten and twenty percent!

"My pastor says we need to be salt and light." While your children can be salt and light in some ways, they are restricted by law in other ways. There are many recent examples of teachers and children who have been sanctioned for attempting to witness. Why can't we find some legal, less dangerous, less harmful, less costly ways to be "salt and light" to our community? But perhaps what is most important to consider is whether your children are old enough, mature enough, or bold enough to be salt and light. Are they ready yet or do they still need training? The truth is that most Christian children are far more influenced by their teachers and peers at school than they are salt and light. The salt and light argument with reference to children is a straw man argument. Consider this: Jesus didn't send His disciples into the world until they were ready and they were grown men!

Jesus told His disciples to follow Him while He showed them how to follow God. This is beautiful thing! As we assume the responsibility that God has given us, we begin to grow. We begin to fail. We begin to repent. We ask God to help us and He does!

Jesus told us to count the cost. He told the rich young ruler to sell all he had, give it to the poor, and follow Him. Jesus also told the rich young ruler that he would have greater treasure than that which he gave away. Discipling your child is costly. But, the treasure you gain is far more valuable.

Chapter Seven

The Most Important Gift to Children: Your Time

Busyness: The Thief of Family Memories

"Seventeen summers" said the busy father, wistfully describing the memory of his oldest child growing up. He continued, "We get seventeen summer vacations and then our children are gone." Is that all there is with parenting; seventeen family vacations? If Scripture teaches that children are a blessing, why am I not enjoying that blessing?

Think about the typical committed, American, Christian's weekly schedule. Father and mother work Monday through Friday. Children spend the day at school or daycare. Monday nights are dedicated to Deacons meetings or ladies Bible study. Tuesday night is church visitation. Wednesday night is prayer meeting with youth and children's activities. On Friday night there is usually a youth activity and/or the parents have a date night. Saturday is for ball games, yard work, and church adult social events. On Sunday morning it's out the door to Sunday School and worship with the children in children's church. It's then home for a quick lunch and nap and then back to the church by 5:00 pm for everyone's separate discipleship class and evening worship. Sunday nights after church are either spent with other church members out to eat or getting children ready for school the next day as its now getting pretty late. On most week nights dinner is on the run between school activities, ball practice, music lessons, and the aforementioned church activities. The one night a week that may not be booked is usually spent with dad in front of the television, the kids on the internet, and mom working on her community or school volunteer project or just keeping up with all the latest on Facebook. Virtually every activity actually divides families. The "treadmill" that we are on is a thief of one of the greatest blessings of God; time with our children. In every arena of our lives our relationships with others are usually just superficial and our busyness contributes to superficial relationships with our children!

You have probably heard the statement that nobody gets to the end of their life and says, "I sure wish I had spent more time at work;" or "I should have spent more time watching television;" or "I wish I had made more money." What do people say? They say, "I wish I had spent more time with my loved ones." Even the respected evangelist Billy Graham said that if he could do it over again he would spend more time with his family. But this problem is not unique to famous people like Dr. Graham. Most Americans can identify with this problem; it is a sign of the times. The problem is that we are too busy to see it.

Doug Phillips, president of Vision Forum asks this question, "Does a fish know that it is wet?" We answer, "Of course not. The fish has always lived in water. It is all the fish has ever known."[15] This is a good analogy of our condition; we don't realize that we are soaking wet with busyness, with keeping up with the Jones, and with being consumed by things that have little long term value. The end result is that our relationships with others suffer.

As a parent you have to figure out that which has the greatest value and that which will bring you the best memories. Training up your children has great value and showing them how to live can change the world. The Deuteronomy 6:7 verse we mentioned earlier, "You shall teach them (God's words) diligently to your children, and shall talk of them when you sit in your house, when you walk by the way, when you lie down, and when you rise up," is written to fathers. God used that verse to arrest me in my tracks. I realized that in all my busyness and in all our activities I could not obey this command.

Even in Jesus' earthly life we have a good example of parental training. Joseph personally taught Jesus the trade of carpentry. Although Jesus may have learned a few things from Jewish scholars (and vice-versa), the primary responsibility for His training was assumed by Joseph. Of course, there is a sense in which we can make some application to ourselves from the relationship that Jesus had with His Father in Heaven. "For the Father loves the Son and shows Him all things that He himself does" (John 5:20).

Today the Melton family lives in the quiet, rural community of Landrum, South Carolina. I work out of my home and my children help me with tasks I need to get done. I teach them things I've learned. Now that we disciple our children, the focus on God is acute and even their SAT scores have improved! My wife enjoys "relearning" as she teaches most of the academics. We have ministry projects we do as a family as our purpose is to be salt and light to our community. Now most evenings are spent together as a family. As I am writing I am drawn to the wonderful, familiar aroma of a home cooked meal and the delightful sound of laughter. Each evening we sing hymns, read and talk about the Bible, and pray together. I tell my children stories of how God has worked in my life. We get together with other families for fellowship.

Our schedule was much like the typical Christian family described previously. We've made a significant change in our lifestyle. Was this an easy change? No way! We have been far outside of our comfort zone. Our family income is much lower. I have been challenged to find a job that I can do from our home. Our drive time to the grocery store is now twenty-five minutes instead of ten. Our children protested our move and our oldest child resented our decision for a while. The children were bored at first as we slowed down, unplugged, and made other changes. We miss our friends. I gave up golf. Living together has required many adjustments from each family member. Our new lifestyle is in stark contrast with the status quo of the American culture.

However, we now see what a blessing our children are. We are making new friends. We already have some new memories together; busyness could never buy what we have now! My wife loves her role as a Proverbs 31 woman. Our children are growing academically as well as spiritually and they are involved in ministry rather than programs. Proverbs 13:20 says, "Those who walk with the wise will become wise, but the companion of fools will be destroyed." Since our children now spend more time with their parents than with other children (the biblical characterization of all children is fools), we have more influence in their lives. Now that I know my children better I can see their individual strengths and weaknesses. I am much better prepared to advise them about their future calling and vocation. Our time together is starting to yield some sweet fruit! We have simply trusted the Lord and He is honoring His word. God certainly doesn't command you to do exactly what we have done, but you need to think about the time, or lack of time, you are spending with your children.

Jesus was with His Disciples

Jesus was not merely with His disciples in His spare time. Mark 3:14 says, "Then He appointed twelve, that they might <u>be with Him</u> and that He might send them out to preach." The idea of "Quality Time" is one of the great lies of our times; our "microwave" approach to discipleship is not working. Like our Lord, parents who disciple like Jesus will sacrifice time, careers, hobbies, prestige, money, entertainment, and possessions in order to be with their children. "Quantity Time" is what it takes to build deep relationships. Jesus said to His disciples, "If anyone desires to come after Me, let him deny himself, and take up his cross, and follow Me. For whoever desires to save his life will lose it, but whoever loses his life for My sake will find it" (Matthew 16:24-25). Are you willing to lose your life in order to follow Jesus and disciple your children?

Divide and Conquer; the Oldest Trick in the Book

Jesus spent a significant amount of time with His disciples. One of the oldest tricks in the book is to "Divide and Conquer." Dating back to the Roman Empire, military leaders used this strategy to erode relationships within the opposition and to foster distrust within enemy camps in order to defeat them. If the Roman military could weaken the internal relationships of the opposition, then a less unified opponent would be easy to conquer. We see this strategy used in today's military operations.

The same strategy was used in the garden by the author of confusion. In Genesis 3, the serpent approached Eve separate from her husband Adam and was able to deceive her. When Adam appeared on the scene he joined her in her sin.

Today this very same insidious strategy is employed by Satan in order to destroy our children. A child simply needs to be separated from the protection of the family and stealing his/her purity and beliefs is as easy a taking candy from a baby.

At the core of the divide and conquer strategy is the erosion of relationships. Parents send their children to be trained and educated by a multitude of others and the time that otherwise would have been used to develop those deep relationships is lost. This dynamic divides the family in a multitude of ways as can be readily seen in our culture.

Children and adults spend a massive amount of time being entertained. In most of the common forms, this practice does not foster relationships; it divides families. I can sit with my family for hours watching movies but I am not really with them nor am I making disciples of them. I am not growing my relationship with them. I can be in my home with my family but that does not mean that I am making disciples of them. I can be on the telephone, reading the newspaper, on the internet, or reading a book, but that is not making disciples.

What is the result of being in the home but not building a relationship with your children? They spend time bonding with their peers rather than with you. The activities mentioned make up the majority of time that could be available to nurture family relationships but the time is lost. The result is superficial family relationships and in many cases relationships outside the home are stronger than within the home. The family is divided and in the perfect position to be conquered.

Unfortunately, the same thing is occurring in many churches. The husband goes to a men's class, the wife goes to a lady's class, and the children all go to separate classes as well. Even worship time is divided in many cases today as youth have their own contemporary services or sit with one another rather than their families and the children, as noted, go to children's church. Many Christian families are more divided than the world! You can begin to see the strategy of Satan at work in almost every aspect of American culture and we have been blinded to it.

Satan knows Deuteronomy 6 and how Jesus made disciples. He has convinced us to give him our children almost all day long. God wants our families to be unified. Think about what Paul said to the church at Corinth: "Now I plead with you, brethren, by the name of our Lord Jesus Christ, that you all speak the same thing, and that there be no divisions among you, but that you be perfectly joined together in the same mind and in the same judgment" (1 Corinthians 1:10). Factions were ruining the fellowship of the church and breaking it apart. The strife created by a divided family is no less serious. If we were to apply this command to our individual families, Paul is pleading with us in the name of Christ not to be divided. Remember, division begins with separation and a door is opened for Satan to gain a foothold (Ephesians 4:27).

Parents, be encouraged! These family situations need not occur. If you will spend lots of time with your children and develop deep relationships with them you will avoid being divided and conquered. Even if you have a teenager with these problems you can begin to spend time with her today while you ask the Lord to "restore what the locusts have devoured" (Joel 2:25). God will honor your spending lots of time with your children because that's what Jesus did with His disciples.

Parents of grown children, you can be encouraged too! Remember that Jesus made disciples out of adults; these grown men were set in their ways. If you will begin to involve yourself in their lives you can begin a discipling relationship with your grown children. You will have a difficult task that will require much prayer and patience. Depending upon the situation, your advances may be more or less welcomed initially. But, persevere. God is faithful and will honor your efforts because you will be doing what Jesus did with His disciples. You can trust Him to do what is right for your children and what is best for you. And remember, God's glory is your ultimate goal both in terms of what you do and what you want for your children. That means that you will not cease to trust God if things don't go exactly as you would like. It will glorify God to commit yourself to the task and He will glorify Himself as a result.

A Father's Absence from the Home

One of the biggest curses on a family is a father's absence of influence, involvement, and love in the home. The father may travel, work long hours, or be involved in hobbies that remove him from involvement with his family. Rather than being with his family, the father sees his role as simply providing food, shelter, and a good education. Many fathers in the church may add church attendance to their responsibility list but they believe that Christian training is the job of the church.

You may be familiar with the song originally written and performed in the 1970's by Harry Chapin entitled "Cat's in the Cradle." This song (unintentionally) captures the biblical principle of sowing and reaping with particular reference to parents and their failure to spend time with their children.

Cat's in the Cradle
My child arrived just the other day
He came to the world in the usual way
But there were planes to catch and bills to pay
He learned to walk while I was away
And he was talkin' 'fore I knew it, and as he grew
He'd say "I'm gonna be like you dad
You know I'm gonna be like you"

I've long since retired and my son's moved away
I called him up just the other day
I'd like to see you, if you don't mind
He said I'd love to Dad, if I could find the time
You see my new job's a hassle and the kids
have the flu
But it's sure nice talking to you Dad, it's been real
nice talking to you.

And as I hung up the phone it occurred to me
He'd grown up just like me,
my boy was just like me.[16]

The father in this song reaped what he had sown. He had developed a shallow relationship with his son that later bore fruit when the son had no time for his dad. The cycle of negligence within the family continued with the next generation. Sadly, many of us have observed how the brevity of time with our children is a cold reality; we look back and before we know it, they are gone.

The Lord will hold fathers particularly accountable over all others when we stand before Him. The command is given especially to us in Deuteronomy 6 and Ephesians 6:4: "And you, fathers, do not provoke your children to wrath, but bring them up in the training and admonition of the Lord." Mothers are certainly responsible to train their children as well. But, fathers are the ones primarily accountable to God even in terms of what mothers do in this regard.

Quality Time; the Great Parenting Lie of Our Times

This book is written for serious, committed, Christian parents who are doing everything they know to serve the Lord and raise godly children. You and I have seen God work in our lives. We may have done better for our children than was done for us. We pray as a family. After all, we all know that the "family who prays together stays together," right? We believe that if we faithfully serve the Lord, take our families to all the church programs, pray before meals, witness to others, tithe, have a daily quiet time, support the poor, and pray for our families, then God will take care of our children. This is the way to build strong families; families committed to each other and to the Lord, right?

What I have suggested above without intentionally discipling our children and spending time with them will make our families weaker than many un-churched American families! The idea of "Quality Time" has hoodwinked many sincere Christians, and as a result, many of our children and grandchildren are being lost.

Let me explain. We live in a "microwave" society. We expect everything to happen quickly. You name it: fast food, sound bites, fast news, cell phones, the internet, productivity at work, etc. We want our children to keep pace with other children; to be competent, educated, and competitive. However, we also want our children to be saved and to walk with God.

So, in an effort to achieve both, we jump on the "treadmill." Our parenting consists of a wake up call, a quick word of admonishment, and a lecture on the way to school. We take our children to all the youth programs. In the evenings there is time for a prayer before we eat, a little help with homework, and a prayer at bedtime. We say to ourselves, "We are spending quality time with our families." Parents, do you really think that this is enough? If you do, you are deceived! Jesus said in Luke 16:13, "No servant can serve two masters; for either he will hate the one and love the other, or else he will be loyal to the one and despise the other. You cannot serve God and mammon." This lifestyle is why many Christian families are weaker than unchurched families.

"The places where your children spend their time will be what will shape their lives."

There is a saying, "Show me your checkbook and I'll show you your priorities." Jesus said in Matthew 6:21, "For where your treasure is, there your heart will be also." With reference to our children, what Jesus is saying is in essence, "Show me where you and your children spend your time and I'll show you your priorities." The places where your children spend their time will be what will shape their lives. Most of our children's lives are being shaped by influences in the following order: school, internet, Hollywood, peers, sports, church, and in last place, parents.

Let's look at some of the fruit of today's Christian "Quality Time" families;

- By the time a child is in first grade he will have spent more time in front of the television than he will spend with his father for his entire lifetime!
- Teenage rebellion is now considered "normal" in the church.
- Most youth from Christian homes lose their sexual purity before marriage.
- Approximately one out of every two Christian marriages fails.

These statistics are reflective of our society. You will note that every one of these problems is related to poor family relationships; generally this means not enough time together.

Why are the statistics in the church no better? If churches are obedient to God's word, why is the fruit of the church the same as the world's fruit? Scripture admonishes us in Galatians 6:7, "Do not be deceived, God is not mocked; for whatever a man sows, that he will also reap." Again, the problem is that parents are ignoring God's command, "You shall teach them diligently to your children, and shall talk of them when you sit in your house, when you walk by the way, when you lie down, and when you rise up" (Deuteronomy 6:7). The fact is that "Quantity Time" is necessary to obey this command of God and to build relationships with your family. The best news is that spending quantity time with our families and obeying the word of God will reduce and possibly eliminate every one of the terrible fruits listed above!

Take a serious look at your family's activities. Do you need to eliminate or greatly reduce outside schooling, entertainment/secular music, time with peers, competitive sports, and age segregated activities? Can you find other activities, ministries, and fellowships that keep your family together?

The more hours you spend with your children, the better. Being with them helps you to earn the right (with them at a subjective level) to be an influence in their lives. Otherwise, someone else is earning that right whether it is a peer, a member of the opposite sex, or Hollywood.

Remember, in the blink of an eye your children will be gone and on their own. Wouldn't it be nice to know that you have obeyed God in making disciples and that your children and grandchildren love the Lord and are your best friends for life?

Chapter Eight

Your Home:
A Discipling Community

Relationships, the Great Theme of the Bible

Needless to say, being with your children is the biggest element in developing a relationship with them. When we read the Bible in its entirety, there is one thing that flows through it from Genesis to Revelation: God's plan of redeeming people so that they might be in relationship with Him. The theme of relationships in the human sphere flows from that dynamic. The Bible is about our relationships with God and with man. Jesus summed it all up when asked about the greatest commandment:

> You shall love the Lord your God with all your heart, with all your soul, and with all your mind. This is the first and great commandment. And the second is like it: You shall love your neighbor as yourself. On these two commandments hang all the Law and the Prophets (Matthew 22:37-40).

We are commanded throughout Scripture to love others. Parents who are serious about making disciples like Jesus did will make relationships with their children a priority.

Of all the relationships on earth, none is more important than the marriage relationship which flows into a relationship with our children. Further, God the Father loves His Son and had face to face fellowship with Him in eternity past. On this earth, Jesus frequently talked to His heavenly Father. In the same way, God gives us a natural love for our children. We naturally want to be with our children; to nurture, feed, cuddle, and protect. But somehow the world has trained us to abandon our children on the altar of culturally generated pursuits. The Bible says,

> Behold, children are a heritage from the Lord, the fruit of the womb is a reward. Like arrows in the hand of a warrior, so are the children of one's youth. Happy is the man who has his quiver full of them; they shall not be ashamed, but shall speak with their enemies in the gate (Psalm 127:3-5).

Although God clearly states that our children are a blessing, we are trained by our culture to think that they are a curse. We believe children are inconvenient. We believe children are costly. And we are right! But because of our self-centeredness, we miss the blessing that could be ours.

What is happening with family relationships is a self-fulfilling prophecy. Since we believe the lie of the devil and send them to be trained by others, the natural result is children that respect others rather than their parents. Since we spend little time with them, the natural result is that children don't want to be with family. Since we don't disciple them, the natural result is children that believe what the world is teaching them. Since we allow them to go out alone into the world, the natural result is children that are devoured by wolves. The fruit of our poor relationships is simply what we have sown.

But the opposite is also true. If you will commit to be with your children and to personally teach them and protect them according to Scripture, you will build deep, lifelong relationships

Being "Real" With Our Children

Sometimes we as parents want to give the impression that we have all the answers, that we don't make mistakes, and that we don't sin. We reason that in order to teach we must know everything. We believe that in order to help our children avoid mistakes we must hide our mistakes. We think that in order to help our children avoid sin we must hide our own sins. But, Peter says, "He who would love life and see good days, let him refrain his tongue from evil, and his lips from speaking deceit" (1 Peter 3:10). He is saying, in one sense, that we must be real with our children.

Being "real" with our children pays huge dividends! As we admit that we don't know some things, our children realize that there will always be things that we don't know and that's alright. As we admit that we too make mistakes, our children understand that none of us is perfect. As we confess our sins to our children, they realize that "all have sinned and fall short of the glory of God" (Romans 3:23), and that we all need a Savior.

Being real with our children helps us to develop a deeper relationship with them. They see us as we struggle through issues. They learn from our example as we show them how to learn, how to move on from our failures, and how to repent and receive forgiveness for our sins.

Mindless Entertainment vs. Hobbies for Relationship Building

Being real necessitates a few words about entertainment. Our family enjoys watching a carefully selected video from time to time. We also love Christian music. Our children have a few video games. While enjoying entertainment is not in itself wrong, we need to ask ourselves some questions about the content and the amount of entertainment in which we indulge ourselves. The ultimate litmus test is this question; "Is this movie, music, show, or game glorifying to the Lord?" If not, believers need to simply say "no."

Consider too that while we may be in close physical proximity with our loved ones when we engage in certain forms of mindless entertainment, this activity does not facilitate the development of relationships with one another. Rather than creating our own stories and experiences with one another we enter the world of the entertainers; they attract us and persuade us to individually enter into their stories. We end up living vicariously through others. If we spend a lot of time in the entertainer's world we are robbed of time with our loved ones and the experiences and stories that would have been our own.

A personal hobby can divide your family. If you are spending a lot of time on a hobby away from your children, consider involving them or giving it up for a season.

On the other hand, a hobby can also give your family something fun to do together. There are scores of things that you can do as a family. Remember when activities were free or cost little? These are the best kind! Hiking, fishing, camping, and cookouts are a few outdoor activities that come to mind. Time spent as a family in nature provides all kinds of ways to impart biblical values through teaching about the Lord. Outdoor games such as basketball, kickball, croquet, Frisbee, tag, hop scotch, hide and seek, and jump rope are a few ideas. Indoor activities can include board games, reading stories together, ping pong, foosball, puzzles, coloring, drawing, and crafts. Choose activities that the entire family can do together and look for opportunities to talk about the Lord while you are together. If you have small children who would not be able to compete with games, play as teams.

Creating Community in your Home

You can set a fine example and teach God's word faithfully to your children, but without a sense of community, your teaching will be hindered. It is this sense of community that is foundational to and creates a discipling atmosphere.

Children need to know they are fully accepted, loved, wanted, and appreciated by their parents. If children feel such only when they do "good," i.e. please their parents, then they will sense a conditional relationship which will not foster trust and the discipling process could be weakened. Jesus modeled a deep sense of love and acceptance for His disciples even when they disappointed Him or did not fully grasp what He was communicating to them.

That is not to say that you should not discipline them when they do wrong. Biblical discipline is never done out of anger but always out of love. Tell your children that you love them as you administer discipline. You discipline them because you love them. As you communicate that reality to them they will know that they are loved and that there are indeed consequences to sin. But, the consequences are for a loving, redemptive purpose. The discipling community thrives in an atmosphere of love and acceptance.

Let's think further here. A few years ago "a father shocked students in a high school biology class by calling his daughter out of her seat and spanking her after learning she had disrupted the class."[17] While corporeal discipline is a biblical necessity at times, spanking a high school age daughter in front of her peer group at school would more likely lead to further rebellion rather than drive it away. A sense of community will not be created that way! This child would more than likely want to get out of the family if this type of thing were a regular occurrence. Parents must be careful to deal with their children in such a way that glorifies God and produces the desired result.

With great concern for all relationships within the body of Christ, in Colossians 3:21, Paul has a word for the fathers. In general, fathers are responsible for the well being of their families. They are responsible for the spiritual atmosphere and emotional climate of the home. Fathers must set the example by treating their children with love and respect. Paul simply says, "Fathers, provoke not your children to anger, lest they be discouraged." Obviously, this admonition would apply to fathers and mothers alike, but the primary responsibility remains with the father.

One who disciples like Jesus and creates an atmosphere of love will not embitter his children. The primary way fathers do so is through hypocrisy. Thus, you must practice what you preach and strive to live according to Christ. If you sin against your child, you must confess your sin to that child and seek forgiveness and reconciliation as you would with anyone else. You must not be inconsistent, harsh, or unfair. As noted, you must discipline out of love and not out of anger.

You must pray for your children without ceasing. God is the only one who can change their hearts and bring them from spiritual death to spiritual life. Pray for your children that you might demonstrate your dependence upon God, that God might be gracious in answering your prayer, that God might save your children, and that God might get the glory, rather than you for so-called good parenting skills. Praying for your children is also an act of love.

"You must pray for your children without ceasing."

Further, you should create an atmosphere in which obedience is natural or easy. As your children receive positive, biblical instruction from you as loving fathers/parents, an atmosphere conducive to obedience is fostered rather than hindered.

Paul says that the result of provoking your children will be their discouragement. Their spirits will be broken. They will lose heart. They will begin to feel as if they can never do anything right or anything that is pleasing to you. Other feelings will mount and the resulting spiritual direction will be different for each child. Some will slip into depression or despair. Others will become angry at life in general. For some, increasing rebellion will ensue. Regardless of the specific direction in which a child goes, the problem is discouragement from a parent who is harsh, hypocritical, or unjust. The power of Christ will not be on display in the child's life as the power of Christ is not operative in the discipline or action of the parent. Rather, the child's spirit will be crushed and/or the Spirit will be quenched. The flame will be doused. Community will be lost.

No parent is perfect. Regarding the incident in biology class cited above, "the girl's mother told the Journal Sentinel it was an isolated incident and her daughter 'comes from a very loving family.' The incident was blown out of proportion and 'the school handled it just fine,' she said, describing the spanking as a 'misjudgment' for which the family apologized."[18] Isolated incidents happen. Let us hope the mother is right on this one. Even children who come from "a very loving family" can be provoked to bitterness toward their parents if their parents consistently act in an unbiblical fashion toward them. An apology to the school was appropriate. Yet, if this father would seek forgiveness from his daughter, not only would that act be more appropriate, but it would go a long way toward demonstrating to her that while we are all indeed sinners, Christ convicts and sanctifies us. Responding biblically to his failure of provocation would give this father a greater platform from which to parent his daughter as she sees the redemptive power of Christ on display in his life. He would be acting like a member of a loving community from which he needs love and forgiveness and in which she too may find the same.

How to Create a Community of Love

We noted that teaching God's word divorced from the context of a loving home community would cause problems. Writing to the church at Corinth, Paul said something similar when he affirmed the emptiness and worthlessness of ministry without love: "If I speak with the tongues of men and of angels, but do not have love, I have become a noisy gong or a clanging cymbal" (1 Corinthians 13:1). Without love, none of the gifts that one may exercise are of value. Thus, Paul moves to describe what biblical love truly is: love is patient, kind, not jealous, does not brag, is not arrogant, does not behave indecently, does not seek its own things, does not become irritated, does not keep a record of wrongs, covers all things, believes all things, hopes all things, and endures all things (4-5). You must develop a community of love in your home in order to disciple your children like Jesus.

Are you patient with your children? The patience to which Paul refers is the patience one exhibits when wronged. It refers to a forbearance regarding offences, slights, injuries, or insults from others. The individual who loves in this way is slow to anger and unwilling to retaliate. His duty and delight is to endure the ill-will of others.

Parents and children alike often are wronged and feel wronged even in the context of their own homes. The remedy for such is patience. How often are you impatient with your children simply because they inconvenience you in some way? If you make a habit of snapping at them for any reason they will get the idea that they are not loved. And, in a biblical sense, they will be right.

If love is patient, then it does not become irritated. When love is on display, one's anger is under control. One's emotion is in check. You will be tempted to become irritated at your children on many occasions. You must fight that temptation by faith. God says you are not loving them if you are irritated with them.

On the positive side, are you kind? Strife, arrogance, and division can permeate a home. You must be considerate of one another, even your children. Tenderness should be on display as opposed to ugliness. You should strive to be helpful rather than hurtful toward one another. What a blessing it is to have your children know that you are a kind person. Not only will you be setting the example, but you will be creating community.

Remember too that love is not jealous. Love does not wish ill-will upon another nor does it desire to have what rightfully belongs to another. These are things that must not only be taught to our children, but demonstrated. Would your children say you were a jealous or covetous person? Are you bitter about your finances when you think of those better off than you? Are you jealous of the time your spouse must spend with your children? Young fathers need to be particularly careful here as young mothers must spend a great deal of time with small children.

The issue is one of focus. Your focus is not to be on yourself but on God and the other persons in your home. So, if love is not jealous, neither does love boast. One who brags is seeking personal recognition. The one who brags is filled with pride and thinks himself more important than others. Moreover, Christ and His glory have been set aside for the glory of the individual. Make sure that your children know that they are just as important as you; in fact, more so! This is why Paul says that love does not seek its own things. Your children will respond when you are selfless when it comes to their well-being.

That means love is not arrogant. This heart issue is connected with the preceding ones. The one who brags does so because he is arrogant. He is prideful. Arrogance is on display when one claims superiority over others. Certainly parents have authority over children. However, you must never lord your authority over them. You must exercise it in love for their good.

You must strive for a home in which all family members behave in appropriate ways toward one another because love behaves decently. A father must be careful not to offend his teenage daughter. She will be more sensitive to certain things than him and there are certain lines that must not be crossed. As a small example, knock rather than barge in, for a number of reasons, when your sixteen-year-old daughter's door is closed.

Moreover, it is indecent for Christians to look down on others. It is indecent for Christians to usurp authority over others and not fulfill the roles that God has given them. Women may not dishonor their husbands nor may they usurp authority in the home. Husbands must love their wives and treat them as the precious jewels that they are. They may never lord themselves over their wives. Whatever the relationship, the one who loves will act decently.

At the same time, you must not keep a record of wrongs. Don't charge sin to the account of others in meticulous fashion like an accountant who records financial information. Some people are able to produce an itemized list of wrongs they have suffered. Yet, Paul says that the one who loves does not keep score or bring up things from the past. The one who loves is quick to forgive.

Children need parents who separate their children's deeds from their worth as God's creation. Some of the greatest opportunities for teaching and discipling your children will come when they have failed you or God: when they have sinned. Living in a relationship and an atmosphere of grace and forgiveness will motivate them to follow more closely. Jesus always forgave His disciples and doing that built a stronger desire in them to learn His ways.

The one who is quick to forgive does not rejoice in evil, but rejoices in the truth. Love does not delight in nor look for fault in others. Love looks at sin in the world and grieves over it. Love does not create mischief for others. Rather, love looks for that which is good and true. Love recognizes the truth that all are in need of redemption. The one who loves is redemptive in all his relationships especially in his relationships with his children.

Being redemptive means that you understand that love covers all things. Family members will regularly sin against one another because they are fallen creatures in the context of a shared environment. In that environment, "love covers a multitude of sins" (1 Peter 4:8). If one is sinned against, it is a loving thing to overlook the offense. As love throws a covering over sin, forgiveness is granted and a relationship is spared from breach. You will have to overlook the shortcomings and sins of others (unless loving confrontation is necessitated according to biblical principles).

Now, love is not naive. Yet, in the context of Christian family and union, it believes all things in the sense that the one who loves takes people at their word. The one who loves believes the best about others. He will not assume the worst, even though an individual's track record may indicate otherwise. You must believe your children. When you do they will know they are part of a loving community. The one who loves will not easily believe unfounded gossip or vicious slander. Love leads to faith, primarily in the grace of God at work in the lives of her children. You need to believe that God is at work in your midst. That is why you will hope all things. Love and faith produce hope. Christian hope is an assurance of God's promises being fulfilled.

When you have hope you will then endure all things. The one who loves is willing to bear all things. He is indeed patient and kind. He has such love in his heart from the Lord that he bears up under the load of wrongs suffered. He bears up under the load of positive action toward others, even those who demonstrate they deserve no such loving treatment. You must build a community of love. The reward will be a loving home for you and your children.

Children Received

Children need an atmosphere of receptiveness in which to be discipled. To be receptive is to be Christ-like to our children. It was Jesus who said, "Let the little children come unto me" (Matthew 19:14). Jesus always had time for His disciples. He likewise always had time for children. Do we sometimes make our children feel they are not important because we do not have time for them? It is one thing to teach that Scripture and biblical values are important, but it is another thing to teach our children that they are important to us and to God. Creating an atmosphere of receptiveness means that you are open and welcoming of your children's questions, problems, and their very presence anytime. If we teach our children that their interruptions are not welcomed, then the open, loving atmosphere and relationship can be damaged. How free do you think your children are to come to you with any problem or question at any time? Build an atmosphere of receptiveness!

Creating this trusting, loving, welcoming relationship and atmosphere takes time and effort but will be most rewarding. Your children will have a sense of belonging.

They will be part of a community. They will have little need to seek community elsewhere. We were created to live in relationship with one another. Part of discipling your children like Jesus is to understand that and take the necessary steps to create a community in which they are safe.

Here are some questions you might ask yourself and your children to help evaluate your home community and its atmosphere:

- Does it feel good to you to live in your family now?
- Are you living with friends?
- Are you living with people you like and trust? Do they like and trust you?
- Are you loved and cared for in your family?
- Does it feel safe and secure in your family?

If you will create the kind of community highlighted herein, your children will be more likely to continue to follow the Lord because you will be discipling like Jesus discipled!

Part IV

Jesus Constantly Taught Scripture and Showed His Disciples How to Minister

Chapter Nine

Teaching Scripture to Your Children

Ayoung man I know was called upon to deliver a morning devotion to his teammates from a Christian school on an away trip. He was excited to have been selected to speak as God had been working in his life for some time. As he stood before the group, he hesitated. He waited. He waited some more. He then turned to the coach and inquired, "What should I say?" Now the coach saved the day and his team- mates were very forgiving. But we sometimes find ourselves in a similar situation even in front of our families.

Jesus spent His three years in ministry constantly teaching His disciples Scripture and how to minister to others. That was His number one priority. In the Great Commission Jesus tells us to teach our children to practice all the things that He has commanded. But, what are we to do if we have been never trained to teach? How can we get the skills we need to do the job well? How can we avoid standing before our families and thinking, "What should I say?"

Building Your "Teaching Muscle"

On the job training is the best way to get equipped! We have the great opportunity and privilege to grow with the rest of our family. Our ability to teach is like a muscle. If we exercise this muscle it will grow bigger and stronger.

Begin with simply reading Scripture aloud to your family each day. Don't worry about teaching anything. Reading God's word is sufficient in itself to bring about dramatic spiritual growth in your family. Ask the Lord to teach you all when you read. Here's what will likely happen as you take a step of obedience in reading to your family.

- The Holy Spirit will begin to bring thoughts to you as you read; from time to time you may be compelled to make a comment about what you have just read.
- If you read and study the Scripture in advance of your time with your family the Lord will give you more to teach.
- If you use a Study Bible to prepare, you will have even more to teach!

Over time as you read God's word to your family you will get better and better at expounding on what you have read. You will become more confident in your teaching ability. The word of God is more powerful than a two-edged sword. You can ask questions about what you just read. As you begin to expound upon God's word all you need to do is to stay one lesson ahead of your children.

What If I Don't Know the Answers to Questions From My Family?

This fear may be the biggest for a new teacher. The concern is how can I teach when I don't have all the knowledge to teach? This concern is a misconception related to our society's expectation that only professionals are qualified to do certain jobs.

If this fear grips you, join the crowd! Nobody knows all the answers to God's truths, not even seminary trained pastors. Simply tell your family the truth; "I don't know." From that point, you have several options.

- As a family you can search for scriptural answers on the spot.
- You can promise to personally check on it and get back to your family the next day with an answer. Then you can search out Scripture, talk with a pastor or friend, or you can "Google" the question. You will need to be careful to select a trusted source on the web; there are many false teachings out there!
- Different family members can look in Scripture and then answer the question the next day during devotions.
- If there is a disagreement about a point in Scripture, those in disagreement can search for biblical proof of their position and then bring their answers back to the family the next day.
- Only God knows the answers to some questions. We have to acknowledge that God is God and we are not. If we knew the answer to every question, then we would be God!

If you take the time to prepare before you teach, you will be able to answer most questions.

Discipleship from Cradle to Grave

There are some who advocate the practice of discipling in certain areas at a certain phase in a person's life. They advocate that during the first few years parents should only focus on training their children to obey. Then over the next few years, they say that parents should focus on catechizing their children or teaching them scriptural meanings. The next few years would be spent on discipleship (as defined by putting the knowledge into practice) of the older children. Then, when the children depart the home the job is finished. This approach is logical; without proper obedience training, the child will not be able to be taught; without biblical knowledge being imparted, the older child will not have a biblical basis with which to operate.

However, Jesus used an integrated approach to discipleship. Jesus did not train His disciples in phases. He did not provide different levels of training to the men based on their age. Jesus took men of different ages from a variety backgrounds and trained, taught, and discipled them simultaneously.

So what are the implications for parents? "When I was my father's son, tender and the only one in the sight of my mother, he also taught me, and said to me: 'Let your heart retain my words; keep my commands, and live" (Proverbs 4:4-5). The Proverb shows the young child being taught and admonished at an early age by his father. Discipleship is for life; from cradle to grave. Think of your children as disciples from birth, even before birth! Pray for them, read Scripture to them, sing to them, and as they grow, take them with you as you minister to others. Give them a foundation from the beginning of what the Christian walk is all about.

"Discipleship is for life; from cradle to grave."

Don't stop discipling your children when they are on their own. Be there for them when they need counsel. Become their chief cheerleader. Confront them when necessary. Pray for them and ask them to pray for you. If your children are now grown and you did not properly train them to obey, prayerfully acknowledge your mistakes and ask them to forgive you. Show them in Scripture how important it is to honor their parents; obedience comes with a promise; long life and well-being. Let them know that honoring their parents is more for their own good than yours. If you did not teach Scripture to them, once again, prayerfully ask for their forgiveness. Ask your children to join you in a regular Bible study (if they live out of town you may be able to engage them in the Word over the phone). You could start by the two of you reading a book and each discussing what the Lord is showing you.

Look for opportunities to minister with your children. If your child has a ministry, offer to help. If not, discuss what people groups and needs she would be interested in meeting. Start a ministry together!

Daily Family Worship/Devotions

If there was only one thing I could recommend to parents it would be to conduct family worship (or devotions) at least daily. Some families have devotions more than once per day. As we read God's word aloud to our families, the Holy Spirit works in our lives. As we sing praises to the Lord, God is glorified. As we pray together for one another and for others we are unified in our spiritual purpose. Of course, God answers prayer as well.

Consider what happened in the Melton family. I am not a big talker; unless I have something specific to talk about, I can go for long periods of time without opening my mouth. I have observed others who just naturally take things from everyday life and apply scriptural principles in a spontaneous teaching. This is the way Jesus taught. But I don't naturally have this gift.

However, at the Lord's leading, I began to teach my children the Bible on a daily basis. We began in the book of Proverbs because I wanted my children to learn wisdom. I used a Study Bible to prepare in the mornings during my quiet time. I would simply read and re-read a verse at a time and then read the study notes until I found some principles that I wanted to explain as I taught through Proverbs. Sometimes I would have a testimony of how a Proverb had impacted my life. At other times I would bring a truth that the Lord showed me. Sometimes I would bring a truth that I found in the notes of my study Bible. Many times I would ask my children what they thought the Proverb was saying. Not only were my children learning Scripture but they were also learning grammar as we discussed the meaning and usage of the words.

Initially I taught Scripture only at home once per day. Then we began to have daily family worship and then over time we began to have our family worship in all kinds of places and settings; in our car, at the park, at a chapel, or in a hotel room. Since studying the Bible has become a regular part of our lives, we find ourselves discussing biblical truths frequently during the day. Now this habit is simply a part of our lives! We naturally discuss the Lord and minister to and pray for others at various times during the day. Recently, each one of us has been bringing a Scripture and a teaching to the family during our devotion time. We have been blessed by watching the powerful word of God transform all of our lives. And it all began by simply reading the Bible aloud. I still have to work at teaching. I still miss the mark some days. I have to be intentional. But the Lord has equipped me to do better.

When children are young, your messages will be brief. Then as children get older, you can add more time and bring more "meat" to them.

Another positive fruit that happens when we read God's word is that the Lord has a way of calming our hearts. Arguments and strife that existed before family worship begins will quickly dissipate as we worship the Lord and focus on Him. Are your children at each other's throats? Begin singing a hymn, reading God's word, and begin praying for God's peace. This peace will give you an opportunity to bring Scripture and teach about how to love one another.

The Power of Our Words

You are teaching all the time by word and deed. Let's focus on the word here. We'll take up deeds a little later. The Lord has given you an incredible opportunity to make a positive impact on your children through your words. "Pleasant words are like a honeycomb, sweetness to the soul and health to the bones" (Proverbs 16:24). "There is one who speaks like the piercings of a sword, but the tongue of the wise promotes health" (Proverbs 12:18). Your words can change lives! They can cause someone who is discouraged to have a change of attitude. "A word fitly spoken is like apples of gold in settings of silver" (Proverbs 25:11). Your words can lead others to eternal life. You can speak life to your children and place your children on the path of righteousness.

On the other hand, your words can destroy. The words that we use can make us unfit to serve the Lord. Scripture shows us that our words can literally lead to death. "Death and life are in the power of the tongue, and those who love it will eat its fruit" (Proverbs 18:21). The "death" part of this verse reminds me of a woman who said vicious things about a teenage girl through a social networking site and the girl committed suicide. How much better it is to heed the "life" part of the verse; again, you can speak words that lead to life.

Jesus reminded us that we will be held accountable for the things we say to others: "But I say to you that for every idle word men may speak, they will give account of it in the day of judgment" (Matthew 12:36). He made it clear that we are not to allow careless speech to flow from our mouths. Parents, more than anyone else, you have the power to shape lives through the words you speak to your children. You can lay a foundation in your children's lives that will make them a blessing to many.

We must also be careful not to allow ourselves to talk incessantly. When we talk without thinking we are apt to say things that are wrong in one way or another. Proverbs 10:19 says, "In the multitude of words sin is not lacking, but he who restrains his lips is wise." We should speak sparingly rather than just carelessly spew out sinful speech. Paul admonishes us to eliminate filthy language: "But now you yourselves are to put off all these: anger, wrath, malice, blasphemy, filthy language out of your mouth" (Colossians 3:8). Further, we must build others up: "Let no corrupt word proceed out of your mouth, but what is good for necessary edification, that it may impart grace to the hearers" (Ephesians 4:29). Finally, James 1:26 is a blunt reminder that if we do not control our tongue our very faith is of no value: "If anyone among you thinks he is religious, and does not bridle his tongue but deceives his own heart, this one's religion is useless."

So, on the one hand we are commanded to teach our children, but on the other hand, we are to guard our tongues. How can we do both? By teaching Scripture! The more we speak and teach the word of God and the less we speak in our own strength, the more our listeners are edified.

God's word brings clarity and purpose to our children's lives. God's word is a lamp to their feet and a light to their path (Psalm 119:105). As we read and ponder the word of God He shows us how to live. "Trust in the Lord with all your heart, and lean not on your own understanding; in all your ways acknowledge Him, and He shall direct your paths" (Proverbs 3:5-6). As we trust, lean on, and acknowledge God, He will give us the direction that we need to teach. God says, "I will instruct you and teach you in the way you should go; I will guide you with My eye" (Proverbs 32:8).

Words are an important key to right relationships with others. Our ability to communicate effectively will foster or hinder relationships.

Words are Important to God

The term "word" or "words" is used over 1200 times in Scripture. Fathers are commanded to train and admonish their children; this requires thoughtful words to get the job done. The wrong words will arouse anger in children but the right ones will produce the fruit of righteousness. "And you, fathers, do not provoke your children to wrath, but bring them up in the training and admonition of the Lord." (Ephesians 6:4) Moreover, children are commanded to listen to the words of their fathers and to obey the rules set by mothers: "My son, hear the instruction of your father, and do not forsake the law of your mother" (Proverbs 1:8).

Perhaps the most important part of teaching our children is the tone we use in speaking to them. "The wise in heart are called discerning, and pleasant words promote instruction" (Proverbs 16:21). Voice inflection can change the entire meaning of a sentence. As we kindly talk with our children their hearts will become open to what we have to say. If our child is angry we can diffuse the situation by talking softly. "A soft answer turns away wrath, but a harsh word stirs up anger" (Proverbs 15:1). Not only that, our body language and facial expression can influence our ability to teach. If I am distracted while I talk with my child he will think I am not interested. If I do not make eye contact he may think that what I am saying is not important. If I "spew out" anger to my child he may not be open to my instruction. We must be diligent about giving pleasant words to our children. Paul compared himself to a faithful father who not only has been given the duty to carry out the task but who was also caring and compassionate toward is children: ". . . as you know how we exhorted, and comforted, and charged every one of you, as a father does his own children" (1 Thessalonians 2:11). If we speak pleasantly to our children, if we show them that we love them, and if we discern the best teaching opportunities, our instruction will have the maximum impact.

Finding the right words at the right time is hard work. I am not very good at this. I can recall times when I was on my knees weeping for my shortcomings with my daughter and asking the Lord to make things right. There have been other times when I was up beyond midnight with my son praying and discussing issues of the heart. In the end, you can count on God to help you and override your failures if you will diligently seek Him in the way you speak to your children.

Asking Questions

When you teach your children you must ask questions to determine whether or not they understand what you are saying. At the same time, real communication takes place when a dialog exists. Who wants to be "preached at?" We all want to be heard and understood.

To foster dialog, open ended questions are the best; questions that cannot be answered by a simple "yes" or "no." Asking questions brings all kinds of information to us so that we may bring a message that is most effective. Again, we can ask questions to understand the level of our child's knowledge. We can ask questions to discern the condition of our child's heart. We can ask questions to draw our child's attention into the conversation. "Counsel in the heart of man is like deep water, but a man of understanding will draw it out" (Proverbs 20:5).

"Who wants to be preached at?"

We can spout off facts about the Bible but our child may not be listening. She may be distracted, hurt, or angry. Our words may have little impact if we do not first understand our listeners. "He who answers a matter before he hears it, it is folly and shame to him" (Proverbs 18:13). Jesus was a master at asking questions. He asked questions of His disciples, the Pharisees, the High Priest, and Pilate. Asking questions first will dramatically improve your ability to teach and enable you to more effectively disciple like Jesus.

Really Hearing What Your Child is Saying

Of course, after we ask questions, we will be getting valuable information. What will we do with this information? Will we be distracted doing other things? Will we interrupt our child before he is finished? Will we jump to a conclusion and overreact to her answer?

When our children speak to us, as busy as we may be, we need to give them our attention. Before you is a great opportunity to draw your child out by asking more questions. Keep asking until you get to the issues of his heart.

Engaging your children takes time and effort. Further, if you have a large family and all your children want to talk with you at the same time, that situation will also be difficult. However, many discussions are great as a group. You may instruct your children to raise their hands to speak and answer their questions as they come one at a time. You may want to set aside a time for each child to ask and answer questions, perhaps as you are putting them each to bed. If you have older children ask them to care for the little ones for a few minutes while you talk with the one in need. Ask your spouse to join you with these conversations.

Here's a good place to start when a question or concern comes your way; begin by repeating what your child has said to you and confirm that you understand the question. Being heard is a big part of good communication; the fact that someone cares enough to understand how we feel goes a long way. Once you have clearly heard your child you are better prepared to give him an edifying answer.

Answering Questions and Concerns

Most of us don't like to be questioned. The person who is asking questions is usually the one in control of the conversation. We don't like being controlled. Sometimes we feel like we are being interrogated. Sometimes we are tired. Sometimes the questions don't make sense. It can be hard work answering questions.

But when our children are asking the questions, this is one of the greatest opportunities and blessings that we can have as a parent! Our child asking questions is a great sign. It is a sign that she wants to learn from us. This is the best time to teach. This is the time to give our child our full attention and turn the conversation to God. Please don't let those opportunities go by.

Conversely, if your child is not asking you questions, you should be concerned. The lack of questions speaks loudly! Now you will need to work hard to draw your child out. You may need to ask forgiveness about something. You may need to spend some one-on-one time with this child. You may need to find out where your child is getting her answers. In summary, the more dialog you have with your child, the better your relationship will be with her.

Allowing Children to Teach

We have alluded to the fact that we as teachers get so much out of teaching through the preparation that is required. Once we are proficient in teaching, why not give our children this gift? Allowing your children to teach will allow you to teach them how to prepare and how to deliver. This too is part of discipleship. They will gain knowledge and skills as they study the Bible and explain its truths. Teaching requires us to process and integrate information. Your children will grow in their logic and their speaking skills.

We've already noted that less than ten percent of all Christians have a biblical worldview. One of the most powerful ways of helping your children to solidify their beliefs is to let them teach what they believe. This practice will pay rich dividends in your child's life, not the least of which is equipping him to communicate the gospel well to others. You will see the labor of your teaching come to fruition in their lives and you will be blessed indeed.

Chapter Ten

The Ministry of Saturation

S wimming is a popular activity in some areas. There are competitive programs for people of all ages. Interestingly, something dramatic happens to a very few persons who swim on a regular basis. All of their hair falls out! We're talking head, arms, and legs. They experience the effects of being saturated with something that isn't good for them. At the same time, their skin becomes completely dried out. But, as they apply good lotion, the harsh effects of the pool water are countermanded. So too, being saturated with the world leads to death while being saturated with the Word leads to life.

Making it Happen

How do you create the life of joy for you and your children? In other words, how can you begin to get a specific handle on discipling your children like Jesus in terms of the Word? Remember, we're laying one leaf on top of another. The principles we've talked about and alluded to must be implemented in a practical way. Let's take a look at Deuteronomy 6:1-8:

Now this is the commandment, and these are the statutes and judgments which the LORD your God has commanded to teach you, that you may observe them in the land which you are crossing over to possess, that you may fear the LORD your God, to keep all His statutes and His commandments which I command you, you and your son and your grandson, all the days of your life, and that your days may be prolonged. Therefore hear, O Israel, and be careful to observe it, that it may be well with you, and that you may multiply greatly as the LORD God of your fathers has promised you-'a land flowing with milk and honey. Hear, O Israel: The LORD our God, the LORD is one! You shall love the LORD your God with all your heart, with all your soul, and with all your strength. And these words which I command you today shall be in your heart. You shall teach them diligently to your children, and shall talk of them when you sit in your house, when you walk by the way, when you lie down, and when you rise up. You shall bind them as a sign on your hand, and they shall be as frontlets between your eyes. You shall write them on the doorposts of your house and on your gates.

While the commands of Deuteronomy were given to the nation of Israel in the context of God's covenant with them, there is tremendous application for us as the people of God. What is said here is foundational to holy living, wholesome family life, and indeed effective parenting. The real issue has to do with glorifying God, or being God-centered in every area of your life. Don't ever overlook that reality, especially when it comes to discipling your children.

Remember your Goal toward God

As a God-centered parent, you must remember your goals. Initially, you have a goal toward God Himself. Think about what God's word says here:

> Now this is the commandment...which the LORD your God has commanded to teach you...that you may fear the LORD your God, to keep all His statutes and His commandments which I command you, you and your son and your grandson, all the days of your life, and that your days may be prolonged.

Your supreme goal must be to fear or reverence the Lord by virtue of who He is as holy. If you reverence Him then you will obey Him and you will do so with joy because your reverence comes from your heart. The result of obedience is a prolonging of your days.

What does it mean to prolong your days? Here you must remember that earthly blessings were promised to Israel under the Old Covenant while the blessings that we have under the New Covenant are primarily spiritual. You have been given every spiritual blessing in heavenly places in Christ Jesus" (Ephesians 1:3). That does not mean that God does not give you earthly blessings; it simply means that the real issue for believers is spiritual. Thus, the New Covenant application of prolonged days is the abundant life that Christ gives to His people. That abundant life is wrapped up in eternal life in Him. You not only have a home in heaven with Jesus, but you have a fullness of life here and now; you have a joy that cannot be shaken no matter what the circumstances (if your focus is on Him); and you have an acute awareness of that which is ultimate. The wonderful blessing for you is that when you reverence and obey God, He gets the glory and you get the joy because nothing thrills the believer's soul like seeing God glorified. Isn't that the essence of your goal toward God in all things; that you glorify Him (1 Corinthians 10:31)?

Your Goal toward your Family

Now, think about your family and the fact that you have a goal toward them as well. You do indeed want to enjoy His abundant life and a long life with your family if the Lord grants. Regardless of whether your lives are long or short, the primary issue is enjoying that which God has given you. Needless to say, when your children are rebellious, you are not experiencing a joy-filled life. You can certainly have a peace and joy in the wisdom and grace of God as He works all things for your good, but you miss out on temporal happiness with regard to your children. At the same time, when your children are rebellious, it may be because you have not discipled them. Be encouraged. There is forgiveness and the life of joy in this context flows from obeying God by way of training your children.

You want to enjoy spiritual success in the lives of your children. That's the application of Deuteronomy 6:3 to your life: "Therefore hear, O Israel, and be careful to observe it, that it may be well with you, and that you may multiply greatly as the LORD God of your fathers has promised you — a land flowing with milk and honey." You must be careful, or filled with care, to observe God's means of discipling your children that it may be well with you and that God may multiply spiritual blessings to you and your children.

I was talking with a young lady in her early twenties not too long ago. Her father is a pastor and had taken a stand on some biblical issues that cost him dearly. I said to her, "I appreciate your father's stance." She responded by saying, "I don't really know what my father believes." This girl's father is a pastor and she doesn't know what he believes.

One would think that a pastor would know how to disciple his children.

The reality is that we are too influenced by the busyness and values of our culture. Too many of us have never even considered that there is something wrong with simply praying at meal time and going to church. How tragic it is to be a warrior for the Lord and fail to train your own children. What about you? Do you see the importance of God's word here? It is your responsibility to intentionally train your children. Who will train them if you don't? Remember your goal: to reverence the Lord by obeying Him in your family life for His glory, your joy and the joy of your family.

If you Love God, You will Train your Children

Did you know that obedience flows from love? That's why it's so important to love the Lord above all things, including your children. In Deuteronomy 6:4-5 we read, "Hear, O Israel: The LORD our God, the LORD is one! You shall love the LORD your God with all your heart, with all your soul, and with all your strength." Based upon your knowledge of who God is, the One True and Living God, you are commanded to love Him with all your heart, soul, and strength. You say, "I certainly know that!" But, practically, what does loving God that way look like?

In biblical terms, the heart and the mind are essentially the same thing. You are to love God with your mind. You are to think about Him and His goodness toward you; His magnificence as God; His power as Creator; His grace as your Savior; etc. Paul says that those who live according to the Spirit set their minds of the things of God, that is, they constantly think about God (Romans 8:5). You are also to love Him with all your soul, that is, with every fiber of your being. You are to love Him with all your strength, that is, with every effort in living a life that is well pleasing to Him.

Jesus said that the one who loves Him is the one who obeys Him" (1 John 2:3-6). Choosing to obey God or disobey God is always a love issue. Do you love God enough to obey Him when it comes to your children? Do you trust Him and His instruction with your children? Do you love your children enough to follow God when it comes to them?

"Your children must see that Christ is your priority"

As a God-centered parent, you must train your children God's way. Let's think about how to go about that training in a general sense.

Your Heart for God is the Starting Point

In the first place, you must train your children from the heart. Everything begins in the heart because all of your thoughts, words, and actions flow from whatever is in your heart (Proverbs 4:23). In v. 6 we are told, "And these words which I command you today shall be in your heart." You must have Christ and His word in your heart if you are to disciple your children. Your walk with Christ must be real and it must be a priority in your life. Your children must see that. Your children must see that Christ is your priority; that you are willing to forsake worldly pursuits for a better satisfaction in Him; that you are willing to love as He loved; that you are willing to confess your sins and seek forgiveness when you do sin; etc.

Further, it is a contradiction to send your children to church and not be involved in church or in their lives yourself. Your goal is not mere moral training. While you want your children to be moral, without Christ morality will send them to Hell. And, statistically, we have seen that without Christ, somewhere along the way, morality goes out the window as ninety percent of our children walk away from Christ when they hit college.

A woman was excited to convey to me that she had her son in church. She allowed him to pick the church for them both. He liked the rock and roll music in the morning service. She commented that she didn't care what church they attended. It was a good thing her son was in church.

Think about that sentiment. What church? What do they teach at that church? What influences are being brought to bear upon her child? Is she involved in his life? Is she discipling him? I referred to her comment as a sentiment for a reason. She, like so many others in the church today, is gripped with sentimentality. Good feelings about being in church will not change a child's heart. At one level it is a good thing to be in church. At another level it means nothing if the child is not being discipled unto Christ. The Scripture calls you as a parent to train your children in God's word, not allow them to pick a church you know nothing about simply because it makes you feel good. This woman has a heart problem. On the one hand, she wants her children to be around good influences. But, she doesn't have a heart for God. She's not loving God with all of her heart, soul, and strength. She is simply floating through life and will one day, sadly, wonder what went wrong with her son if he walks away. If you are going to be what you need to be for your children, it begins with your heart.

If you Love God, You will be Diligent

In the second place, train your children with great diligence. Because we live in a fallen world and because all of us have been affected by that fall, child rearing is not easy, and that's an understatement! Add to that the dynamic of discipleship and the task becomes that much more difficult. Every effort will be required; but, in the end, the effort will be worth the result. God tells you to do something with His commands (Word): "You shall teach them diligently to your children, and shall talk of them when you sit in your house, when you walk by the way, when you lie down, and when you rise up" (v. 7).

God says you shall teach your children. Teaching has to do with communicating the truth about God to your children and making specific application of that truth to their hearts. In one sense, teaching is discipleship. Jesus commanded you to make disciples by baptizing and teaching them to obey everything He commanded. Teaching to obey involves the application of God's Word to the heart. Paul wrote: "All Scripture is given by inspiration of God and is profitable for doctrine, for reproof, for correction, and for instruction in righteousness, that the man of God may be complete, thoroughly equipped for every good work" (2 Timothy 3:16-17). Teaching involves equipping your children for every good work.

The Bible says that it is the Word of God which sanctifies your children" (John 17:17). James wrote: "Therefore lay aside all filthiness and overflow of wickedness, and receive with meekness the implanted word, which is able to save your souls" (James 1:21). If the only "information" your children ever receive is the first principles of the gospel or a mere application of those principles time and again, they will never be discipled and will actually be in spiritual danger. They are likely to remain unconverted like so many in the American church today.

The Bible issues a strong warning in this regard. The writer to the Hebrews exhorted:

> Therefore, leaving the discussion of the elementary principles of Christ, let us go on to perfection, not laying again the foundation of repentance from dead works and of faith toward God, of the doctrine of

baptisms, of laying on of hands, of resurrection of the dead, and of eternal judgment. And this we will do if God permits. For it is impossible for those who were once enlightened, and have tasted the heavenly gift, and have become partakers of the Holy Spirit, and have tasted the good word of God and the powers of the age to come, if they fall away, to renew them again to repentance, since they crucify again for themselves the Son of God, and put Him to an open shame (Hebrews 6:1-6).

Teaching your children more than the basics is critically important.

The Ministry of Saturation

Now, a hit and miss approach to teaching is not good enough. God says you are to teach your children constantly: "when you sit in your house, when you walk by the way, when you lie down, and when you rise up" (v. 7). God is not giving a schedule for us to follow in a legalistic sense. He is saying that you must take every opportunity to speak to your children about Him and His word. Rather than spending hours watching television, you must talk to your children about God. When you are out walking or riding in the car, perhaps on the way to school or soccer practice, you can take the opportunity to talk to your children about God. At supper, after supper, before you go to bed, when you get up in the morning and have breakfast, talk to your children about God. That's a lot of talk about God! But that is the point. You must diligently make the most of everyday opportunities to point your children to Christ.

Isn't that what Jesus did with His disciples? When they were walking down the road He saw a wheat field and took the opportunity to tell them about the Kingdom of God.

When they were hungry on the Sabbath He told them about Himself. When they were looking at the temple He took the opportunity to tell them about His death. Jesus made the most of the time He had with His disciples. You must make the most of the time you have with your children. You won't be perfect and you will miss many opportunities. But, with an understanding of Jesus' method and with a little bit of intentionality on your part, you will begin to delight in talking to your children about the things of God on a regular basis. You will begin to make connections between the world and God that you never saw. And, you will be diligently teaching your children.

Children are like sponges. They soak up everything around them. If you keep God's word before them, they will soak it up. You will be engaged in the ministry of saturation! The wonderful part is that God uses His word to change the hearts of your children. That's why Paul says that not being conformed to this world and being transformed into the image of Christ comes through the renewing of the mind" (Romans 12:3). How do you renew the minds of your children? Saturate them with God's word "when you sit in your house, when you walk by the way, when you lie down, and when you rise up" (v. 7).

God also says something else about His commands (word): "You shall bind them as a sign on your hand, and they shall be as frontlets between your eyes. You shall write them on the doorposts of your house and on your gates" (vv. 8-9). God is giving us a picture here. His word is to be so much a part of your life and the lives of your children; it is to be so evident as to who you follow and what you're about; that it will be like having a Bible tied to your hand, or pasted between your eyes, or written all over your house. The picture is one of saturation! We might say it like this: God's word should be all over you and your children like talent is all over Michael Jordan!

Much more needs to be said in terms of "how to" apply God's word to the hearts and lives of your children. But, in bringing this chapter to a close, I want you to remember one thing: the ministry of saturation. I want you to diligently saturate your children with God's word "when you sit in your house, when you walk by the way, when you lie down, and when you rise up."

Chapter Eleven

Applying God's Word to your Child's Heart

What would you say to your five-year-old if he came into the house with his clothes completely covered in mud? You would tell him to take the dirty clothes off and put on some clean clothes. But before putting on the clean clothes you would tell him to take a bath. It doesn't do much good for a child merely to take off muddy clothes nor does it do much good to put clean clothes over a muddy body; they won't really be clean then! So it is with sin. We must put off sin. But, it's not good enough to do that. We must then put on righteousness and the only way we can do that is through a renewed mind.

Put-off/Put-on and Renew the Mind

You know your children. But, God is the One who knows how to change your children. That's why it is so important to disciple your children like Jesus. You have already seen that you must diligently saturate your children with God's word "when you sit in your house, when you walk by the way, when you lie down, and when you rise up" (Deuteronomy

6:7). That means you will talk to your children about God a lot. But, what does that talk look like? Is there a way to get a handle on some specifics in terms of applying God's word to the hearts and lives of your children? While that talk will include a great many things, remember, dealing with the hearts of your children is primary because everything flows from the heart" (Proverbs 4:23). Even Jesus said, "But those things which proceed out of the mouth come from the heart, and they defile a man. For out of the heart proceed evil thoughts, murders, adulteries, fornications, thefts, false witness, blasphemies" (Matthew 15:18-19).

In discipling your children like Jesus, one of the things you must do is confront their failures and shortcomings from a biblical perspective" (Matthew 7:1-5). Your goal is to enable your children to turn their focus from self and their desires to that which is well pleasing to God. A commitment to the Lordship of Christ and the authority of His word is critical if biblical change is to occur. Paul wrote:

> For this reason also, since the day we heard of it, we have not ceased to pray for you and to ask that you may be filled with the knowledge of His will in all spiritual wisdom and understanding, so that you may walk in a manner worthy of the Lord, to please Him in all respects, bearing fruit in every good work an increasing in the knowledge of God; . . . (Colossians 1:9-10).

As your children are filled with the knowledge of God and His wisdom, they will be enabled to live in such a way as to please Him in all respects.

Now, you can teach your children to obey the commands of God through a very simple formula found throughout Scripture in a variety of forms. The formula involves replacing ungodly habit patterns with godly habit patterns.

The replacement of habit patterns is accomplished through renewal of the mind. Both sides of the equation and renewal are necessary for true heart and habit transformation to take place.[19]

Your child needs to learn to be responsible for his own behavior. In learning that responsibility, your child needs to understand the conflict between his old self and his new nature in Christ. Your child must determine, by an act of his will, to lay aside his old way of life with its lusts and deception and to begin to act in a way that reflects the new Christ-like nature God has given him.

"Pour God's word into your children"

What if you have a child who is not yet converted? The Bible says that you are to teach your children to obey God whether they are converted or not. You must deal with their hearts just as you would deal with your own heart. At the same time, you must pray that God brings about the necessary heart change. Further, as you train your children from a young age, they grow up with a commitment to God whether the new birth has occurred or not. Now, don't misunderstand. Your goal is for your young children to one day believe on Christ by virtue of God's work in their lives. They are not saved simply because they have your commitment to God. But, never forget that it is God's word that is His power unto salvation" (Romans 1:16). Pour God's word into your children; deal with their hearts; pray; teach them to obey; and trust God for the results.

Right Thinking Produces Right Living

Commit this biblical principle to memory: right thinking will produce right living. A genuine renewing of the mind is necessary to fulfill the actions of putting off sin and putting on righteousness from the heart. Paul wrote:

> . . . that you put off, concerning your former conduct, the old man which grows corrupt according to the deceitful lusts, and be renewed in the spirit of your mind, and that you put on the new man which was created according to God, in true righteousness and holiness. Therefore, putting away lying, "Let each one of you speak truth with his neighbor," for we are members of one another. "Be angry, and do not sin": do not let the sun go down on your wrath, nor give place to the devil. Let him who stole steal no longer, but rather let him labor, working with his hands what is good, that he may have something to give him who has need. Let no corrupt word proceed out of your mouth, but what is good for necessary edification, that it may impart grace to the hearers. And do not grieve the Holy Spirit of God, by whom you were sealed for the day of redemption. Let all bitterness, wrath, anger, clamor, and evil speaking be put away from you, with all malice. And be kind to one another, tenderhearted, forgiving one another, just as God in Christ forgave you (Ephesians 4:22-32).

Note Paul's general admonition to "lay aside the old self" and "put on the new self" through "being renewed in the spirit of your mind." Note the specific "put offs" and "put ons." First, put off lying and put on truth speaking. Second, put off stealing and put on labor. Third, put off unwholesome words and put on edifying words. Fourth, put off anger etc., and put on kindness etc.

It's Both/And

Teach your children to put off those things that do not honor God. Don't leave it there however. You must teach them to put on a corresponding behavior pattern that pleases God. When does a liar cease to be a liar? When he stops lying? No, at that point he is simply a liar who is not lying at the moment. A liar ceases to be a liar when he puts on truth telling. Then, if he lies on a particular occasion, he is a truth teller who lied in that moment and needs to repent.

Paul regularly moved from the general formula to specific areas. In Colossians 3:8-14 he wrote:

> But now you yourselves are to put off all these: anger, wrath, malice, blasphemy, filthy language out of your mouth. Do not lie to one another, since you have put off the old man with his deeds, and have put on the new man who is renewed in knowledge according to the image of Him who created him, where there is neither Greek nor Jew, circumcised nor uncircumcised, barbarian, Scythian, slave nor free, but Christ is all and in all. Therefore, as the elect of God, holy and beloved, put on tender mercies, kindness, humility, meekness, longsuffering; bearing with one another, and forgiving one another, if anyone has a complaint against another; even as Christ forgave you, so you also must do. But above all these things put on love, which is the bond of perfection.

Notice his first admonition, "put them all aside" followed by a list of "put offs." In the latter portion of the text, Paul shifts direction with "put on" followed by another list.

At other times, Paul used the same formula with different words as in Romans 12:2: "And do not be conformed to this world, but be transformed by the renewing of your mind, that you may prove what is that good and acceptable and perfect will of God." Instead of put off/put on, or lay aside/put on, Paul gave the formula "be not conformed" but "be transformed" through "the renewing of your mind." The "put off" generally has a corresponding "put on." This habit pattern replacement comes from the heart as the mind is renewed.

Dealing with your Children at the Right Level

Much has been said about change coming from the heart. At the same time, when dealing with your child's heart, you should recognize three levels of every problem.[20] **First, there is the feeling level.** Your child may lack joy or peace. It may be she doesn't feel well. She may feel angry. You should explore those feelings to ascertain the nature of the problem.

Second, there is the doing level. Parent, you need to help your child identify specific thoughts, words, and actions which violate biblical commands or principles. When a child is focused on self, he will allow his feelings to dictate his behavior. If your son hits his sister because she took his truck, or if he throws a tantrum when you tell him its time to put his toys away, his actions flow from a feeling of being wronged in some way. You are taking away from him the most important thing in the world to him in that moment. When based upon feelings alone, decision-making and activity, even for children, often leads to more problems; especially when those feelings are negative! The temper tantrum may lead to a more serious rebellion as you attempt to deal with him.

The Bible clearly teaches that one's behavior should issue forth from a commitment to please God through obedience to His word. God blesses those who obey Him regardless of feelings. Ultimately, good feelings will come as God produces His fruit in the life of your child. The point is that you must help your child to understand who God is and how to lead a life that is pleasing to Him. You can do that when you understand what's going on in your child's heart. It always comes back to that issue.

Third then as noted, there is the heart level. Jesus said: "But the things that proceed out of the mouth come from the heart, and those defile the man. For out of the heart come evil thoughts, murders, adulteries, fornications, thefts, false witness, slanders" (Matthew 15:18-19). The way your children respond to their problems is a reflection of that which is in their hearts. While human beings cannot look upon the heart, and cannot even understand their own hearts, (Jeremiah 17:9) God can and does. He examines the human heart and enables persons, including you and your children, to examine their own hearts in light of His Word" (Hebrews 4:12). You as a parent must trust the Holy Spirit by the Word to pinpoint the sin that lurks in your child's heart. You trust the Holy Spirit as the true changer of hearts to bring about the desire and ability to change.

Thus, discipling your children in this way of applying God's word to their hearts, in simple terms, involves putting off unrighteous habit patterns and replacing them with godly habit patterns. This process is accomplished through the renewing of the mind that the behavioral change might flow from the heart. Mere outward conformity to the law does not please God, nor does it bring about ultimate transformation, but only temporary relief through external, behavioral change. You and your children must understand their problems at the feeling, doing, and heart levels if you are to deal with their hearts in such a way as to bring about God-pleasing change. That is why you constantly point them to Christ and their need for Him to help them love Him and what is right. Behavior is not the issue: love for Christ is. Behavior will follow.

A Closer Look at Discipling Unconverted Children

You do need to understand who your children are apart from Christ. Again, behavior change is not your ultimate goal. Nor can you let good behavior deceive you into thinking your child is converted if there is no real heart for God. Your ultimate goal is the gladness of your child as she is drawn into a relationship with God.

As the result of Adam's sin, all human beings including your children, are born in sin and are by nature spiritually dead (Eph. 2:1-3). God had placed Adam in the garden and warned him not to eat of the tree of the knowledge of good and evil on the threat of spiritual death (Genesis 2:16-17). Adam sinned, and in so doing, brought spiritual death upon all human beings (Romans 5:12).

Paul affirmed, "As it is written: 'There is none righteous, no, not one; there is none who understands; there is none who seeks after God. They have all turned aside; they have together become unprofitable; there is none who does good, no, not one' (Romans 3:10-12. He stated: "But the natural man does not receive the things of the Spirit of God; for they are foolishness to him, nor can he know them, because they are spiritually discerned" (1 Corinthians 2:14). David confessed: "Behold, I was brought forth in iniquity, and in sin my mother conceived me" (Psalm 51:5).

As the result of the fall, your unconverted children are blind to spiritual truth, their hearts are desperately wicked, and their minds are foolish and darkened (Romans 1:18-32). The Bible teaches that human beings are born dead in sin and are in need of a new birth if they are to be brought from spiritual death to spiritual life (John 3:5-7). Thus, in your training, you must constantly bring the gospel to bear upon the lives of your children.

Think about this for a moment. You must bring the gospel to bear upon the lives of your children even if they are saved!

What if your daughter gets angry on a regular basis? You tell her that anger should be put off and patience or kindness should be put on. She then says to you through angry tears, "I can't keep from getting angry." Do you respond by simply ordering her to stop, getting angry yourself, ignoring her, or by telling her there will be consequences if she doesn't stop? Or do you say something like this: "Honey, I now you can't help getting angry. That's why Jesus died on the cross for our sins. He died to take our sins away and to help us to live in a way that pleases Him. It is only by grace that we can do better. Let's ask Jesus to help you not be angry." That response deals with the sin of anger and also brings the gospel to bear upon your child's heart. This is true whether she is saved or not.

Think further. Unsaved children do not understand the things of God (1 Corinthians 2:14). If your child does not understand or receive the things of God because he regards them as foolish, he will not submit to the authority of Scripture. He will be given over to his own opinion or feeling with regard to his circumstances. He will not be helped immediately or eternally if the gospel is not brought to bear upon his heart.

In another sense, and unsaved child cannot do what she is asked to do. An unbeliever may deem your instruction to be good when she is young or good in certain instances when it suits her whim. But, without the power of the Holy Spirit, her heart will be unaffected by your admonition. She may be able to modify certain behaviors for a time, but she will ultimately fall back into old habit patterns. Thus, you must keep the gospel of Christ before your children.

In a sense, discipling your children includes evangelizing your children. If an unsaved child is evangelized, he has the power to live a God-glorifying life: Christ Himself. Paul wrote:

Beware lest anyone cheat you through philosophy and empty deceit, according to the tradition of men, according to the basic principles of the world, and not according to Christ. For in Him dwells all the fullness of the Godhead bodily; and you are complete in Him (Colossians 2:8-10).

Paul's point is that worldly philosophy is empty deception, vanity, or hollow. Often, it looks substantial and sound. When one embraces the wisdom of the world however, it only crumbles beneath one's feet. Worldly wisdom is after the tradition of men as opposed to the One who created humanity. Philosophy is after the elementary principles of the world as opposed to the infinitely higher principles of the One who created the world. Worldly thinking is not after Christ. Thus, if one falls into the elementary thought patterns of the world, she is kidnapped and taken captive by them. Only in Christ is one complete. If one is to have power for a God-glorifying and joy filled life, she needs Christ, ". . . seeing that His divine power has granted to us everything pertaining to life and godliness, through the true knowledge of Him who called us by His own glory and excellence" (2 Peter 1:3). If your children are to be complete and receive everything they need for life and godliness, you must bring the gospel to bear upon them every day.

Now, you might be overwhelmed at this point. You might think the job is too big for you. It's not too big of a job: God chose you to do it and God is always right!

Chapter Twelve

Showing Your Children How to Minister to Others

Not only did Jesus constantly teach Scripture to His disciples, He also showed them scriptural principles in action. It is one thing to teach theoretical principles. The Pharisees knew the law. But it is something entirely different when the teacher shows by example how Scripture is actually lived out.

What Are We Teaching When We Are Not Teaching?

We noted earlier that we are always teaching by word and deed. We focused on our words; now let's focus briefly on deeds. We are constantly teaching our children whether we are aware of it or not. The question is what are we teaching? When we dent a car in the parking lot and don't leave our contact information, what have we taught? When we lose our temper and curse, what have we taught? When we don't witness to someone who has shared a little of their life with us, what have we taught? When we yell at our child or spouse and don't apologize, what have we taught? When we frequently choose entertainment and rarely choose

159

ministry to others, what have we taught? When we are rude to service people, what have we taught? When we say uncharitable things about others behind their backs, what have we taught?

You may have heard the saying "evangelism is more caught than taught." The same idea is true with teaching in general. Another saying is "our actions speak louder than our words." No matter what we say, our children will follow our actions. Our attitudes, our mannerisms, our countenance, and our voice inflection will be mirrored in our children. Jesus said that you will know a tree by its fruit. Generally speaking, if you want to see your reflection, good or bad, simply examine your children.

Integrating the Bible into Our Lives with Family Ministry

In God's economy, the family plays a specific role. God calls human beings, and indeed Christians, to populate and subdue the earth for His glory and the good of man. He calls you to this task. Your family provides a stabilizing force in an otherwise frenzied society. It is in the context of family that men and women learn the absolute necessity of being responsible adults and the duty upon them to train their children. It is through the family that the gospel is propagated in a visible way as Christ's commitment to His church is magnified in loving relationships and as children are taught to fear the Lord.

There are some tremendous implications for your family in God's command to take dominion over the earth. God has a role for you and your family to walk the road of life together in this regard. It is the individualism of our culture that militates against such an understanding. And yet, God has a specific purpose for families together as families. Certainly we all have different roles within the family. But, those roles must mesh into this dynamic of togetherness if we are to honor God and find maximum fulfillment within our family life.

Now, we are taught by our culture to keep our faith separated from the rest of our lives. The culture tells us that church should have no influence on the state and that we should only practice our faith on Sunday. However, what good is our faith if we ignore it six days out of the week? To the degree that we buy into that message, we are hypocrites. This hypocritical behavior is the opposite of what Jesus commanded us. He told us to "go and make disciples." Disciples practice their faith around the clock.

True disciples integrate Scripture and scriptural principles into their lives. They see all of life through the lens of Scripture. The natural out flowing of integrating the Bible into our lives is our service to God and man. We begin to do what Jesus did!

Another unfortunate problem with many existing ministries is that a lot of them are not designed for family involvement. Instead, ministries are created that separate families. Your children will benefit by serving with you in ministry. After all, that's what Jesus did. He took His disciples into the world for ministry.

"What are you passionate about?"

What are you passionate about? The Lord frequently gives believers a passion about some ministry need. Perhaps the Lord has given you a concern about a certain people group. You may have a heart for starving children, orphans, the unborn, the homeless, people in third world countries, prisoners, juvenile delinquents, disaster victims, the elderly in retirement homes, or children in hospitals. Many ministries are born out of a burden from the Lord about a certain injustice for a people group. Pray about what ministries with which the Lord would have your family to be involved. Helping to provide for the needs of others will frequently open the door for praying, witnessing, and sharing the gospel with them. This will help you and your children to learn about ministry.

The School of Life

Jesus constantly took His disciples out and ministered to others. In so doing, He showed them how to minister to others. You must follow His example and integrate your children into your ministry in different ways.

When I graduated from college over twenty years ago, before I knew exactly what God wanted me to do at the time, my father took me with him everywhere he went. Jerome Dean was a business man. He took me to meetings that involved contract negotiations, troubleshooting, problem resolution, and the general promotion of good will among customers that I might know how he handled these things. He introduced me to bankers, lawyers, accountants, and other professionals that I might not only know them but that I might know when and for what I needed them. Along the way he talked to me about more than his business. He talked to me about how he viewed things and how to handle life in general. He took me with him as he ministered to others in various ways whether it was a long-term project for a church; hospital visitation, crisis care, or benevolent response as a deacon in his church; or the development of long-term rela-tionships with business associates or laborers. He shared his dreams with me concerning kingdom advance and so much more. In a sense, I was his apprentice in the school of life. And though he's been with the Lord for ten years now, my life is still affected on a daily basis by the lessons he taught me in those days. Taking your children with you when you minister is not only an opportunity for ministry but an opportunity for imparting yourself to your children.

Interacting With Your Child in the World

During the three years that Jesus spent with His disciples He was constantly going places with them. They traveled to towns and cities around them and encountered all kinds of people. They went to parties. They fed thousands of people. They preached the gospel. They healed the sick. They raised the dead. They cast out demons. As they went into the world Jesus was living His life *with* them.

As parents and followers of Jesus we are commanded to do the same. We should take our children into the world and show them how to interact, evangelize, and minister to others. It is only as we engage them this way that they will truly understand their callings as believers.

Just prior to His arrest Jesus prayed for His disciples: "I do not pray that You should take them out of the world, but that You should keep them from the evil one" (John 17:15). Jesus was praying for the protection of His disciples because they would be in the world.

While we are to protect our children, the Bible also makes it clear that we are not to isolate ourselves from the world. "A man who isolates himself seeks his own desire; He rages against all wise judgment" (Proverbs 18:1). Many Christians have gotten confused about how we are to act around sinners. Paul clarifies the issue:

I wrote to you in my epistle not to keep company with sexually immoral people. Yet I certainly did not mean with the sexually immoral people of this world, or with the covetous, or extortioners, or idolaters, since then you would need to go out of the world. But now I have written to you not to keep company with anyone named a brother, who is sexually immoral, or covetous, or an idolater, or a reviler, or a drunkard, or an extortioner—not even to eat with such a person (1 Corinthians 5:9-11).

Paul's point was clear: we are to withdraw from believers who habitually sin for redemptive reasons but not the lost. Most importantly, Jesus did not reject sinners either. He constantly was going to them to minister, heal, and save them from eternal damnation.

Parents are to take their children with them into the world to encounter sinners and saints for the purpose of being a light. As the Lord leads we can pray for others, meet the temporal needs of others, witness to others, share the gospel with others, and encourage others. As children see their parents doing what Jesus did they will be encouraged to follow their parents and Jesus.

With a little initiative, ministry can be done together as a family. Simply taking meals to those who have needs creates an opportunity for prayer and compassion. Serving as foster parents gives opportunity to minister to orphans. Helping together in a food distribution ministry demonstrates giving to the poor and sharing of the gospel. Consider church visitation as a family or inviting neighbors over to dinner. Thanksgiving is a great time to take your family to feed the homeless. Show mercy and help other families with projects around their homes.

I know a family that ministers to low level offender prisoners; the entire family goes together at least once per week to share the gospel and to minister in other ways. Another family cares for special needs children. Other families go together on short term mission trips. When there is a disaster such as a hurricane or flood some families will go to provide relief to the victims. Arnold Pent wrote an enjoyable book about his family entitled *Ten P's in a Pod; A Million-Mile*

Journal of the Arnold Pent Family. His book details the life of a family that traveled the country sharing the gospel and living by faith.

Many families practice hospitality by inviting their neighbors over for a meal or other activity. This is one of the most edifying things you can do as a Christian family. Paul says that we should be given to hospitality (Romans 12:13). As you invite others into your home, you enter into the blessed gift of relationships with others. If your guests are believers then this is an opportunity for fellowship, encouragement, and a time for "iron to sharpen iron." If your guests are non-believers then this will be an opportunity to display what a Christian family is like. As you pray before meals, read Scripture and glorify the Lord through testimony, there is a good chance that your guests will be attracted to the Lord. This may lead to opportunities to minister and share the gospel with your guests in the future.

Going Boldly Where We've Never Gone Before

Pray about what God may want you to do with your children in terms of ministry. We should think about being more intentional and expanding the scope of our focus. The Lord Jesus talked about ministering to the "least of these" in prison for example. A plain reading of the gospel accounts demonstrates that our Lord was concerned with the poor, the down and out, and/or the outcasts of society. Think about teaching your children to go where they've never gone before. Jesus did.

While the kingdom of God is something to be ultimately realized in the future, even now it is a present reality. The kingdom is the rule and reign of Christ in the hearts of believers and this world. If the kingdom is a present reality, Christians participate with God in the advancement of that kingdom on earth. That advancement, while including evangelism, includes the transformation of society from the inside out through the power of changed lives.

The love that God demonstrated to His people is a love in action. Paul wrote in Romans 5:8: "But God demonstrates His own love toward us, in that while we were still sinners, Christ died for us." Christians desire to participate in the loving activity of God in this world. May we demonstrate that reality to our children as we demonstrate Christ to others.

Part V

Jesus Sent His Disciples Out in Twos to Protect Them from Wolves

"After these things the Lord appointed seventy others also, and sent them two by two before His face into every city and place where He Himself was about to go..." "Go your way; behold, I send you out as lambs among wolves" (Luke 10:1,3).

Chapter Thirteen

Big Bad Wolves Everywhere

So many dangers and wolves threaten our families; it is wise to dwell on this reality in a focused way. For the sake of ease, we'll place them in five broad categories; wolves that seek to steal our children through philosophy, immorality, technology, entertainment, and predatory means. Some of the dangers we'll mention could fit into more categories than one. For example, various artists or performers via the entertainment industry frequently promote an anti-Christian philosophy through technological venues resulting in an erosion of morals. Some forms of entertainment are promoted by predators who seek to trap their victims. Pornography or certain video games are examples. Hopefully though, separating these issues into different categories will be helpful to you in clarifying the dangers that lurk.

Wolves Attacking through Philosophy

Jesus was concerned that His disciples could get devoured by "wolves" and therefore warned against false teachers. He described how the "leaven" of the Pharisees would ruin the whole person.

Wolves who attack through philosophy are some of the most dangerous and insidious that your child will face. These wolves seek to destroy our Christian worldview and replace it with a secular one; one that lines up with Satan. False worldviews can come at us from any source. All false ideas are fostered by the enemy and we are confronted with them wherever we go. In many arenas we have no control over the information we are receiving; someone else chooses that for us. We are constantly barraged by ideas that have Satan as their author. Consider that a million bits of information every day is aimed at your family and most of it is contrary to Christ.

What is the information saying? It is telling us that sex outside of marriage is good and Christians are evil. It is telling us that Darwinism is right and Christians are stupid. It is telling you that there is no truth. It is telling you that either God does not exist or there are many different kinds of gods that you may follow and they all lead to the same end.

Check out the county library, most any Christian school's library, and even a number of church libraries and you will be surprised to find any number of books focused on the occult, romance, violence, and all kinds of other things contrary to Christ. Many will be written by non-Christians. We certainly want our children to know about other worldviews but we want them filtered through the lens of Scripture. We want the words that they read to be edifying and uplifting. Paul admonished,

> Finally, brethren, whatever things are true, whatever things are noble, whatever things are just, whatever things are pure, whatever things are lovely, whatever things are of good report, if there is any virtue and if there is anything praiseworthy—meditate on these things (Philippians 4:8).

Our children's young minds are shaped by what they see and read. The point is two-fold. First, you are your child's screener; you cannot blindly trust others. Second, you will have to teach your children discernment so that they can begin to screen things for themselves over time as God works in their hearts.

If your children are taught by philosophical wolves, this teaching will bear fruit in their lives. This spiritual reality is why so many Christians are concerned with public education. It is grounded in humanism by design and the manifestations of that worldview, whether subtle or overt, are increasing at breakneck speed. It is critical that you disciple your children one way or another. Jesus told us that a student will become like his teacher.

Perhaps the most dangerous philosophical wolves today are found in secular colleges and universities. It really is no wonder that the second year of college is the year that most youth are leaving the church never to return. Not only do many professors aggressively attack the Christian faith but they also promote other worldviews that are diametrically opposed to the Christian faith.

Reducing exposure to this kind of information is appropriate but teaching the truth in a relevant way is the real key. When you cannot avoid a particular wolf, be sure to warn your children. Encountering a philosophical wolf can become an opportunity to point out the lie and to teach truth to your child. Make sure you are present in your child's life as much as possible and be vigilant to notice and to point out these dangers.

Wolves Attacking Through Immorality

Some other dangerous wolves in our culture attack through immorality. These are the wolves that seek to steal the purity of believers and therefore our testimony and effectiveness in the kingdom. They steal our sight and vision of God's kingdom. Jesus said "Blessed are the pure, for they shall see God" (Matthew 5:8). When parents cannot see things in the spiritual realm they can't adequately train and protect their children. When children cannot see things in the spiritual realm they lose their purity and ability to serve the Lord as well.

Our morals are constantly under attack by the entertainment industry; television and movies regularly show children, teens, and adults engaging in sexual activity. Schools train children that sex is going to happen, so be sure to use protection. Government supported and financially lucrative Planned Parenthood seeks to keep child abortions hidden from parents. Magazines show scantily clad models and the internet has millions of pornographic websites. Television and movies glorify extramarital sex. Secular music constantly hammers us with story after story of unmarried adults and youth who are "doing it." But Scripture tells us that since our bodies are filled with Jesus Christ through His Holy Spirit, we are not to join Him to things that are not holy. Paul reminds us that "Our body is the temple of the Holy Spirit" (1 Corinthians 6:19). We are to honor God with our temple; we are to keep our bodies pure.

"Television and movies glorify extramarital sex."

Peer influence and pressure is a major cause of moral breakdown among children. Since many parents are not discerning about their children's activities, many of your children's peers are trained to be immoral. When a child does not come from a Christian home or when a child comes from a home more influenced by the culture than Christ, these other children can't help but be wolves influenced by Satan. How will you deal with them? Scripture has an answer. Paul says in 1 Corinthians 15:33, "Do not be misled:

"Bad company corrupts good character" (NIV). It is better that your children walk with those who are wise.

So what is the practical application here? The first principle is to limit the amount of influence that other children have on your children. You need to monitor the activity of your children and their friends. Remember, Scripture characterizes all children as fools. "Foolishness is bound up in the heart of a child" (Proverbs 22:15).

The second principle is to maximize your time with your children. Do fun things together with your children: go to parks, go to museums, or go on trips. Let your children walk with you and other Christian adults. Don't be deceived by the world. They will enjoy spending time with you.

This subject is far too important to gloss over. We're talking about God's word and the eternal condition of your child's soul. Salvation is not a matter of simply walking an aisle or mentally accepting Jesus into your heart. It is a total heart and nature change wrought by God. Don't be deceived into thinking your children are saved simply because they know John 3:16 and go to church. Are they bearing fruit? Are you discipling them into Christ?

Because of the eternal significance of what we're talking about here, let me challenge you a bit further. Are you discerning when it comes to the issue of youth groups? Most youth groups are good for lost children and for those from homes whose parents will not train their children. However, biblically speaking, most youth groups are defiling for children from Christian homes. Why? Because when lost or spiritually immature children get together apart from or with weak supervision, their flesh wins out and the conversations and activities turn to things that corrupt. Moreover, and let God's word be your authority, can you find one Scripture or any biblical basis for the practice of youth groups or are they a product of our culture like so many other things we have never thought about? Truthfully, there are plenty of warnings against such a practice in Scripture. If your child must be in a youth group, then make sure you are in the group with her! That's what it means to be involved.

Wolves Attacking Through Technology

The development of the worldwide web has ushered in both an incredible blessing and curse to the Christian world. On the blessing side, we have a wonderful opportunity for gospel advance through the internet in a variety of ways. We can praise God for that.

Unfortunately, there is also a negative side to the internet. There are more dangers related to technology than can be adequately discussed. Here's a timely topic for an aspiring author, "The Dangers of Technology." A Google search will yield over two-million references to that search term!

We are all aware of the myriad of objectionable sites on the web and the filters we can purchase. But that is not enough. Many sites don't get filtered including lingerie sites, store catalogs with the same, and even the news which covers modeling events. A friend of mine has a teenage son that has fallen victim to internet pornography; he had the filters but somehow his son was able to get around them. This addiction has led to excessive web surfing in general. Sadly, this is not an unusual situation. Below are some statistics from SafeFamilies.org;

- As of 2003, there were 1.3 million pornographic websites; 260 million pages *(N2H2, 2003)*.
- U.S. adult DVD/video rentals in 2005: almost 1 billion (Adult Video News).
- Hotel viewership for adult films: 55% *(cbsnews. com)*.

- More than 70% of men from 18 to 34 visit a porno-graphic site in a typical month (comScore Media Metrix).
- More than 20,000 images of child pornography posted online every week (National Society for the Prevention of Cruelty to Children, 10/8/03).
- 51% of pastors say cyber-porn is a possible temp-tation. 37% say it is a current struggle (Christianity Today, Leadership Survey, 12/2001).
- Over half of evangelical pastors admit viewing pornography last year.[22]

We are instructed in 1 Thessalonians 4:7-8: "For God did not call us to uncleanness, but in holiness. Therefore he who rejects this does not reject man, but God, who has also given us His Holy Spirit."

Social Networking, chat rooms, and instant messaging are recent web offerings that are taking the culture by storm; groups like Facebook, MySpace, and other sites have millions of child members who network with one another. Adults and children post photos and personal information which often leads to real connections. Hookups, casual sexual encounters with little or no commitment, are made easier through these networks. Perhaps the biggest danger to children is the predators that surf these networks; adults pose as children and arrange for meetings with children and teen-agers. The results have been kidnappings, rapes, suicides, and murders.

Another recent rage is the use of cell phone cameras. These cameras are used to store photos of friends and busi-ness contacts. Unfortunately, these cameras are an easy way to photograph nudity and sexual activity which is in turn easily downloaded to the internet. This is one of the ways that girls get dates these days; they photograph themselves naked and show the images to prospective hookup partners and boyfriends. Of course this is also an easy way for boys to show off their sexual conquests to their friends.

Allowing your children indiscriminate access to these mediums is putting them in the way of temptation, something God would never do (James 1:13). Let us use technology for God's glory. That means monitoring that usage when it comes to our children.

Wolves Attacking Through Entertainment

CBS News recently reported:

a "...new study is the first to link [television] viewing habits with teen pregnancy, said lead author Anita Chandra, a Rand Corp. behavioral scientist. Teens who watched the raciest shows were twice as likely to become pregnant over the next three years as those who watched few such programs."[23]

Further, violent entertainment contributes to teen violence. According to P2pnet News:

To be published in February, 2009, in the Journal of Youth and Adolescence, the study shows even when other factors such as academic skills, encounters with community violence, or emotional problems, are considered, "childhood and adolescent violent media preferences contributed significantly to the prediction of violence and general aggression.[24]

This is why we are told to "think on things that are pure" (Philippians 4:8f).

You may decide to give up television altogether as some have or simply limit and monitor. You might get rid of cable or purchase a cable filter. While it is possible to watch television for the glory of God, limiting your viewing activity will yield wonderful fruit. You will have more time developing relationships with your family; your conscience will be pricked more when you do watch television as you clear your head of the cultural fog that has subtly closed in; and you will have joy in being set free from a form of bondage to television that has trapped many.

Ultimately, God wants your family not to be polluted from the evil things of the world and he would rather that you spend your time with wholesome family activities and ministering to the less fortunate. Consider these things prayerfully.

Wolves Attacking Through Predatory Means

When Jennifer and Ryan were both preschoolers, they were playing in our cul-de-sac in front of our home. I kept one eye on them while I was picking up sticks in our front/side yard. I noticed a car with an out of state license plate slow down and pull over across the street. The driver got out of the vehicle and started walking toward Jennifer and Ryan. Since there were trees and shrubs in our yard, apparently he did not see me, and he approached my children with a big smile on his face. Suddenly aware of the danger, I jogged toward them and asked him if I could help him. Once he became aware of my presence, he turned and ran to his car and "scratched off" out of the neighborhood! The reality of the situation hit me hard; if I had simply walked into the back yard for a minute, one or both of them would have been gone. I thanked the Lord for His protection, but resolved to personally protect them more closely.

Gangs, child abusers, kidnappers, school and mall shooters, sexual predators, and carjackers are just a few of the big, bad wolves lurking about. It is not unusual to find a sexual predator among extended family, in the neighborhood, or even in church. With seventy percent of men viewing pornography on a regular basis, these fantasies can come to pass with children. In the last few years another disturbing trend is female teachers seducing male students. Organizations that support the abortion industry help young girls to hide from their parents the crime of adults raping children. We see regular notices of child abductions. It's not unusual for most of us to have had some close calls. Even the nursery set up in large churches is a potential danger spot as volunteers often don't know the children or their parents very well.

At the risk of sounding redundant, sexual predators are trolling the internet, malls, pre-schools, schools, neighborhoods, parks, and even churches looking for children that they can use for their own sexual gratification or for a source of income. Once they have a child in their control, they will abuse, photograph, make movies, or torture the child. They may pass a child on to others to do the same or they may kill the child. Sex trafficking of children, according to www. born2fly.com, is happening to one million new children every year.[25] These children are sold up to twenty times per night. In America there are approximately one hundred thousand children between the ages of nine and nineteen that are trafficked every day according to the FBI. By the time these children reach adulthood, they have AIDs or other sexually transmitted diseases.

It sounds so legalistic or fearful to talk about keeping our children with us as much as we can. The need to do such may not have been as great when we were children. However, we live in a fallen world and there is danger around every corner. We have a responsibility to be wise and watchful!

Chapter Fourteen

Keeping the Wolves at Bay

J esus was protective of His disciples. He cared for them. Jesus understood that one of the important strategies of God's plan was to multiply disciples and the process of multiplication would be hindered if He allowed His disciples to be devoured by wolves. So Jesus personally trained them; He did not allow others to do this task. Jesus personally taught them; this task was too important to delegate to others. He personally showed them how to minister and how to live the Christian life. Then, when He sent His disciples out, he sent them out in twos.

> After these things the Lord appointed seventy others also, and sent them two by two before His face into every city and place where He Himself was about to go. Then He said to them, "The harvest truly is great, but the laborers are few; therefore pray the Lord of the harvest to send out laborers into His harvest. Go your way; behold, I send you out as lambs among wolves" (Luke 10:1-3).

The fact that Jesus sent his disciples out in twos would ensure that they would be accountable to one another for their behavior. And, if they encountered wolves, the disciples would have someone to cover their backs.

"Jesus was protective of His disciples."

By using Deuteronomy 6 as His training method, Jesus had built-in assurance that His disciples would be protected. Since He personally taught His disciples, He knew what they were learning. Since Jesus was with them all day long, He was aware when they encountered wolves. Since He was personally teaching them, glorifying God, and showing them how to minister, He didn't have to guess about what they had learned or had not learned.

At the conclusion of His earthly ministry, Jesus prayed for the protection of His disciples: "I do not pray that You should take them out of the world, but that You should keep them from the evil one" (John 17:15). Jesus protected His disciples until the very end. When He was being arrested He once again protected His disciples from the cross that He was about to bear. In John 18:7-9 we read,

> Then He asked them again, "Whom are you seeking?" And they said, "Jesus of Nazareth." Jesus answered, "I have told you that I am He. Therefore, if you seek Me, let these go their way," that the saying might be fulfilled which He spoke, "Of those whom You gave Me I have lost none."

Jesus knew that His disciples would play an important role in building the Kingdom of God from that time forward. The protection of His disciples was crucial to the future fulfillment of the Great Commission.

Parents the Shepherds: Psalm 23

In addition to describing the attributes of our Lord and Savior, this beautiful Psalm teaches us much about how we are to care for and protect our children. We are to protect them like Jesus protected the twelve.

"The Lord is my shepherd; I shall not want." Here we see the provision of the shepherd. Most parents are good at providing food, shelter, and transportation to their children. But what provision do you personally make for your children's spiritual knowledge? What training are you providing in how to interact with others? How are you providing for them in the area of ministry involvement? What is your provision in teaching them to discern good versus evil? Take personal responsibility for not only their temporal needs but also their eternal needs.

"He makes me to lie down in green pastures; He leads me beside the still waters." This verse speaks of rest, nourishment, and refreshment. In the midst of the dizzying pace of our present world, do you provide a place of respite for your family? Do you and your children ever stop to catch your breath in a place of safety, solitude, and peace? When God created the earth, He ordained rest every seven days. How often does your family rest? Do your children have a quiet time with the Lord? Ensure that your family gets rest, refreshment, and time with God.

"He restores my soul; He leads me in the paths of righteousness For His name's sake." Since the fall of Adam and Eve people have needed restoration on a continual basis; we fall off God's path and choose our own. Like sheep we are prone to wander. All of us have sinned and have fallen short of the glory of God and we sin constantly. However, His word tells us that we simply need to confess our sins to be forgiven and restored to fellowship with the Lord (1 John. 1:8). Restoration allows us to get back on the path that our

Lord has placed in front of us. Do you provide loving correction for your children and then restore their souls? Do you forgive and choose not to bring your children's sin before them again? Do you show your children where you have wandered off God's path and then received restoration from the Father? Do you lead them in the path of righteousness? Provide loving restoration to your children and lead them into righteous living.

"Yea, though I walk through the valley of the shadow of death, I will fear no evil; for You are with me; Your rod and Your staff, they comfort me." There is no doubt that in this troubled, fallen world that we all will encounter peril of some sort. Whether the peril is disease, or crime, or temptation, or simply traveling down the road, we and our children are constantly at risk to some degree. We all know that the enemy has come to steal, kill, and destroy. The actions that we take to deal with these perils will determine in large measure whether or not the enemy has victory over our family. The reason that no fear exists in the valley of the shadow of death is the fact that the shepherd is with His sheep and He has some tools at His disposal. The "rod and staff" mentioned here was likely the same tool with different applications. The rod was used to keep the sheep from hurting each other and to keep them within the fold in a place of protection. The staff was used as a weapon to beat back the wolves when they tried to devour the sheep. Parents, are you with your children so that you may protect them? Do you lovingly discipline your children to keep them in the protective care of God's fold? Do you use weapons or strategies to defend your children from the numerous wolves that exist in the world? Be with your children so that you may protect them. Lovingly use the rod and fiercely use the staff.

"You prepare a table before me in the presence of my enemies; You anoint my head with oil; My cup runs over". Shepherds needed to prepare new pastures for their sheep

once the existing pasture had been removed of the grass and foliage by the hungry sheep. The "enemies" included not only wolves but also poisonous weeds. Therefore, the shepherd would "prepare a table" for His flock. The meaning of anoint is associated with blessing; the Shepherd's diligence in preparation is a blessing to His flock. Parents, do you plan in advance the places you will take your children, the activities that they will engage in, the curriculum they will be studying, and the peers they will be associating with? What will your children read, watch, listen to, and engage in? Prepare in advance the environment where your children will live and the influences in which they will be immersed. Create a culture of blessing in your children's lives by your diligent planning and preparation.

"Surely goodness and mercy shall follow me all the days of my life; and I will dwell in the house of the Lord Forever." Here is the payoff for the faithful Shepherd and His sheep; for the faithful parent and her children. The children and parents will be blessed with mercy and goodness for the length of their lives. Most importantly, they will dwell in the house of the Lord forever. Parents, I know that you want your children to dwell in the house of the Lord forever. You would not be reading this book if you were not concerned about the spiritual condition of your children.

Parents, if you will follow Jesus in the way that you shepherd your children, you can know that you have done everything you can for your children to ensure that the Lord will grant them goodness, mercy, and eternal life. While we can't know with certainty the Lord's sovereign will for our children's lives, we can rest knowing that we have been obedient to His calling.

Jesus was aware of the "Wolves" That Threatened His Disciples

In the days that Jesus walked the earth there were lots of wolves. There were false teachers who could lead His disciples down the wrong path. An ungodly culture existed that could lead His disciples into sin. Jewish leaders could entrap and kill His disciples. But Jesus would not allow this to happen. That doesn't mean that some of His disciples did not lose their lives for the sake of the gospel. Eleven of the original twelve disciples died martyr's deaths. But, it does mean that He protected them spiritually so they would not lose their souls. Of course, He protected them physically until God's providence brought them to death for His glory. For you as a parent, God has called you to protect your children physically and spiritually as best you can. In the end, their lives are in His hands. But, you have a responsibility to fulfill.

As we have seen, today the list of dangers for children is quite large and particularly so when we think of small, unconverted, or spiritually immature children. The effects of the fall in Genesis continue to snowball at a dizzying pace. Again, a partial list of the wolves that our children face today includes unsaved teachers, false teachers, abusive coaches, peers, bullies, gangs, and child predators. Other dangers include: teenage hookups, STD's, pornography, inappropriate movies, unwholesome television shows, secular music, school shootings, mall shootings, violent video games, cell phone cameras, the internet, books (even some "Christian" books), the homosexual agenda, public education, and worldly philosophy. You have probably thought of others that I haven't named here.

Think practically and specifically with me for just a moment. Dr. Russell Moore, Dean of the School of Theology at Southern Baptist Theological Seminary, deals with a common issue for parents today.

> A pre-teen or a teenager with unrestricted cell-phone usage (or Internet or television consumption) is being placed in a very, very difficult place of temptation. The company of that young man or woman is now away from the scrutiny of parents, and is now left only to his or her discretion or conscience. Are there some young Christians who can handle such? Of course. Should you assume your child is one of them? Your Father is more careful of you than that. . . Your responsibility is to know about every call, and the identity of every person text-messaging your son or daughter. You don't have time to monitor this? Then you don't have time for your child to have a cellphone. This doesn't mean you have to turn your house into an Inquisition hall. It simply means your child knows that you love him or her enough to check in frequently to see what's going on in life. . . Communicating your love to your child means communicating your involvement. The gospel message is one of Fatherhood and sonship, of a Father who knows the hairs on our head (Luke 12:7), who fights for his children when they're tested, tempted, or mistreated. Picture that kind of God to your children, even if they grumble and complain at first.[26]

Here we have an example from which principles may be gleaned for other areas in terms of keeping the wolves at bay.

Peter warns us to "Be sober, be vigilant; because your adversary the devil walks about like a roaring lion, seeking whom he may devour (1 Peter 5:8)." Satan is indeed real and you need to be knowledgeable and vigilant about the dangers your children face. Of course, as noted heretofore, the biggest issue is the condition of your child's heart. He will at least have some motivation and weapons to fight dangers and temptations if he knows Christ. But, keep in mind that even Christians can fall and we are told to pray that God would keep us from being tempted for this very reason. On the other hand, if your child does not know God, all the protection in the world won't give him a heart for Christ. Morality apart from Christ is itself a deadly wolf that deceives many straight into Hell. But, as noted, you must protect you children to keep them from temptation and danger to keep them unspotted from this world and ultimately being devoured by Satan. No saved person wants to fall and no person saved later in life rejoices over past sin. Protection is important on so many fronts. Ask the Lord to give you spiritual eyes to see the dangers that exist.

How Parents Can Have "Spiritual Eyes"

Many things can hinder our ability to see and acknowledge dangers that exist for our children. Most parents and grandparents were raised in much less threatening environments. We are tempted to "let our guards down" because we did not personally experience these dangers. We want our children to have the same experiences that we had. Since we lack the discernment necessary (or have a spiritual blindness) to protect our children from present day dangers, many children are lost.

Metaphorically speaking, so many parents sacrifice their children on the altars of our culture. The ancient Ammonites worshipped Molech through child sacrifice. It is hard to imagine anything more horrible than murdering your own child in this way. As abhorrent as that practice may sound, modern parents often do the same thing in different ways. One modern day altar is career; is advancing your career more important than protecting your children? Worldly wealth is another modern day altar; is your stuff more important than protecting your children? Other modern day altars include education, hobbies, status, entertainment, and convenience. Are any of these altars more important to you than protecting your children?

Sin is often passed down from one generation to the next. "The Lord is longsuffering and abundant in mercy, forgiving iniquity and transgression; but He by no means clears the guilty, visiting the iniquity of the fathers on the children to the third and fourth generation" (Numbers 14:18). Most Christians have been raised in a faulty discipleship system. Instead of receiving discipleship in the manner that Jesus made disciples we have been trained in the world's system. We simply do to our children what was done to us. But you can change and bring blessing to your children and their children by discipling like Jesus.

Of course, the greatest thing that blinds parents to the dangers facing their children is sin. Many parents are trapped in the world of pornography, excessive entertainment, or other self-gratifying practices. Rather than dying to self daily, many parents are in bondage to sin in their own lives which causes spiritual blindness. This blindness leaves our lambs vulnerable to wolves! We need to purify our souls in order to answer our high calling. Paul said, "Since you have purified your souls in obeying the truth through the Spirit in sincere love of the brethren, love one another fervently with a pure heart" (Ephesians 5:22). Jesus said, "Blessed are the pure, for they shall see God" (Matthew 5:8). Parents need to be pure in order to shepherd their children.

Many parents are captivated by the same wolves that threaten our children. Parents, if you are trapped in a sin, realize that there is more at stake than just your own spiritual condition. Your children's lives are at stake as well. You are blinded to the wolves in their lives and your children may be devoured. Ask the Lord for grace in your life. Remember, "If we say that we have no sin, we deceive ourselves, and the truth is not in us. If we confess our sins, He is faithful and just to forgive us our sins and to cleanse us from all unrighteousness" (1 John 1:8-9). Once you have become spiritually cleansed, ask the Lord to help you see the dangers that lurk and ask for the wisdom to take up your staff and fight off the wolves with all your strength.

Are You a Good Shepherd For Your Children?

Here I would like to show you another entire chapter in Scripture that describes Jesus as a shepherd. In John 10 we read:

> "Most assuredly, I say to you, he who does not enter the sheepfold by the door, but climbs up some other way, the same is a thief and a robber. But he who enters by the door is the shepherd of the sheep. To him the doorkeeper opens, and the sheep hear his voice; and he calls his own sheep by name and leads them out. And when he brings out his own sheep, he goes before them; and the sheep follow him, for they know his voice. Yet they will by no means follow a stranger, but will flee from him, for they do not know the voice of strangers." Jesus used this illustration, but they did not understand the things which He spoke to them. Then Jesus said to them again, "Most assuredly, I say to you, I am the door of the sheep. All who ever came before Me are thieves and robbers, but the sheep did not hear them. I am the door. If anyone enters by Me, he will be saved, and will go in and out and find pasture. The thief does not come except to steal, and to kill, and to destroy. I have come that they may have life, and that they may

have it more abundantly. I am the good shepherd. The good shepherd gives His life for the sheep. But a hireling, he who is not the shepherd, one who does not own the sheep, sees the wolf coming and leaves the sheep and flees; and the wolf catches the sheep and scatters them. The hireling flees because he is a hireling and does not care about the sheep. I am the good shepherd; and I know My sheep, and am known by My own. As the Father knows Me, even so I know the Father; and I lay down My life for the sheep. And other sheep I have which are not of this fold; them also I must bring, and they will hear My voice; and there will be one flock and one shepherd. Therefore My Father loves Me, because I lay down My life that I may take it again. No one takes it from Me, but I lay it down of Myself. I have power to lay it down, and I have power to take it again. This command I have received from My Father."

Jesus is talking to a crowd of uninformed people, His own disciples, and the Pharisees. The Old Testament background of the text must be understood in order to understand what He is saying. God is the shepherd of Israel and the individual sheep that make up Israel. He is a good and loving shepherd but there are evil shepherds in the world. Sheep are prey when the evil shepherds leave them to the wolves. In one sense, the evil shepherds are wolves themselves. Christ Himself is the Great Shepherd.

We are told in v. 6 that the account is an allegory, that is, an extended metaphor. With such a literary device we must not try to explain every facet or symbol. Of course, when Jesus gives us an interpretation we accept it immediately. We are told that Jesus Himself is the Door. The sheepfold is Israel. The sheep are those for whom Jesus died, those destined to be saved, those who obtain eternal life, and those who heed the voice of Christ and follow Him. Jesus is also the Shepherd. The flock is the entire company of the saved. The thief, robber, stranger, and hireling are the Pharisees. Understand that mixed metaphors are no problem in this type of literature. The point is that Christ is the Good Shepherd and contrasts Himself with the evil shepherds who are the Pharisees. Christ is also the Door but that is a secondary emphasis in this allegory.

Christ is superior to all other would-be shepherds because those other shepherds do not enter by the door. They try to enter or teach others to enter (salvation) by means other than Christ the True Door. They try to enter through works, philosophy, science, relativism, etc. These other shepherds are nothing but thieves and robbers. They seek to steal Christ's sheep and often do so for personal gain. Christ alone is the true shepherd of the sheep. As the true shepherd, the doorkeeper admits Christ into the fold. He calls His own sheep by name. He leads His sheep from the fold. He goes on ahead of His sheep, that is, He leads them. His sheep know His voice and they follow Him. At the same time, Christ's sheep will by no means follow a stranger.

The application for us as parents is that we ultimately point our children to Christ as the only means of life. There are false shepherds or wolves out there who would try to point our children away from Christ to other worldviews or means of salvation. They would steal our children away from us and Christ. We must make sure that our children follow Christ and are able to discern His voice from the voices of strangers who would destroy their souls.

Think about those you allow to care for your children. This could be a babysitter, a nursery, a school, a sports program, and unfortunately, even a relative. You must be careful that these are not hirelings that would spiritually damage your children. I've discovered youth pastors who take young teens out drinking; coaches who physically assault children; one youth pastor I counseled got caught in a motel room with a girl from his youth group. I know someone whose child was molested by an uncle. Remember, Jesus protected His adult disciples, and on the rare occasions that He sent them out without His protection, they went out with trusted adults. When the need arises make sure those you entrust your children to are indeed trustworthy. As noted in a previous chapter, no one cares for your children as much as you.

Your sheep should follow you because they know your voice and of course you must follow Christ. Unfortunately some parents become strangers to their children and therefore so does Christ. They send their children away for most of the day, allow hirelings oversight, and consequently the children begin to follow the voice of those hireling(s), rather than the parents. The thief is stealing those children.

Following Christ as the Good Shepherd means that we parents are willing to lay down our lives for our children. The most important thing you can do is lead your children into abundant life. Only as parents do the things that shepherds do can they protect their children from the wolves. This task cannot be given to the hireling; the hireling is a stranger to your child. He flees when the wolves come and at times he is the wolf.

You shepherd your children by knowing them intimately, keeping their hearts, being present during times of danger, and laying down your life for them on a daily basis. Generally that means giving up personal time and conveniences. But in some rare cases it could literally mean losing your life in defense of your child.

Issues for you to consider have been raised. Only God can give you the specifics of how to protect your children in any given context. Age and spiritual condition will be major factors in your decision-making process. Above all, know the dangers, seek the Lord, pray for your children's spiritual well-being, and pursue the joy and reward that is to be had in protecting your children from the evil one.

Chapter Fifteen

Special Areas of Concern for Older Teens

College

Before thinking about college, think about the kind of education you want for your children. Do you want them to be trained in a worldview that is opposed to Christ? You say "no." You may be thinking like so many others though, "Isn't the education my children need to succeed in life neutral? After all, math is math and science is science." The first problem with that sentiment is that success as defined by the world is not your goal. Success as defined by God is your goal and His definition has nothing to do with the American Dream and everything to do with His glory. The second problem is that there is no neutrality. You either see things from a biblical worldview or the wrong worldview.

For example, math is not just math. In fact, math only makes sense on a biblical worldview. Evolution is rooted in random chance. Two plus two may not be four tomorrow. The reality is that math is predicated upon the fact that God is a God of order and has invested the universe He created with natural law. Two plus two will always be four. God made it that way. On a postmodern worldview two plus two is whatever you want it to be. Of course, such a statement is irrational. So too is education apart from God. What about history? Well, history is His story. God was up to something in the War of 1812 for example. You can't understand that war apart from God. You can understand some facts. But, you can't understand its meaning and the implications in terms of kingdom advance and its real cause and purpose apart from God. You can't understand anything apart from Christ: "In Him are hidden all the treasures of wisdom and knowledge" (Colossians 2:3). All knowledge is rooted in God.

Think just a little further here. One of the basic dynamics that attends any worldview that is contrary to the Christian worldview is a lack of philosophical justification for it. This dynamic holds true even in the realm of simply knowing something to be true. In other words, the unbeliever has no basis for knowing anything.

When an unbeliever makes a statement concerning God, the world, man, morality, ethics, or any other subject, he asserts it as an absolute certainty. For example, an atheist who believes in evolution may say that God does not exist. However, on his worldview, he has no basis to make such a statement. On his worldview, knowledge is obtained through observation (or the scientific method). His problem is that he has limited knowledge and ability to obtain that knowledge. He does not have the ability to search every square inch of the cosmos to determine whether or not there is a God. On his worldview, he cannot know that there is no God. His statement of certainty is rendered completely uncertain.

At the same time, he may then say that we can't know or that we don't know whether or not there is a God. He is agnostic at that point. However, he has asserted a certainty in his mind, namely, that we don't know whether or not there is a God. Again, on his worldview, he is rendered uncertain in that he does not know whether or not there is some kind of knowledge somewhere that can tell us whether or not there is a God. He has not investigated the entirety of the universe on this point. He has no philosophical or logical basis to make such a statement.

Of course, Christians have a basis or a philosophical justification for their assertion that there is a God. On our worldview, we know there is a God because He has revealed Himself to us. We are not bound to the limits of empiricism/ observation. We know that some knowledge is revealed.

At the same time, we can affirm that we don't know everything, nor, must we. We have an explanation as to why we don't know everything. In addition to the fact that God's general revelation takes time to investigate, God has not revealed everything to us: "The secret things belong to the LORD our God, but those things which are revealed belong to us and to our children forever, that we may do all the words of this law" (Deuteronomy 29:29).

What about the issue of goodness? College professors who are humanists will say we should be good. Again, they have no justification for such a statement on their worldview. On their worldview, we are here by accident and therefore have no purpose, no absolute standard of right and wrong, and cease to exist when we die. Without purpose or a standard, it is philosophically inconsistent to say persons should be good. Moreover, who defines "good" on such a worldview? The relativist has the same problems. If there is no standard, no one can define "good" for another. Someone might say our survival depends on being good. Answer: on that worldview, who says survival is good and again, what is being good?

On a Christian worldview, we are specially created by God with purpose and we are given a standard by which to live. What we do in this life matters in eternity. That alone is a rational basis for being good.

"What we do in this life matters in eternity."

God must be an integral part of our education and thinking. You must believe in God to be truly educated.

A belief in God provides the only rational basis for goodness, morality, ethics, or the rule of law. These things make no sense without a universal standard.

A belief in God provides the only rational explanation for metaphysical dynamics like laws of logic, the mind, or language. Where do such immaterial things come from on a naturalistic worldview that says there is no such thing as the immaterial?

A belief in God provides the only rational basis for the scientific method. Such a method presupposes a universe of design and order, not one that came to be by chance.

A belief in God provides the only rational basis for liberty and justice for all. Such things are rooted in the justice of God. Apart from Him, those in power make the rules. Long term freedom for all people can only be sustained in a society rooted in a Christian worldview. When the Christian worldview goes, liberty goes with it.

A belief in God provides the only rational answers to ultimate questions including how we got here, what the purpose and meaning of life is, how we must live, and what happens when we die. Apart from God, individual hedonism and despair are the only logical conclusions.

A belief in God provides the only rational basis to seek salvation for the soul. When one comes face to face with the futility of everything apart from God, he is ready to hear the gospel.

Don't you want an education for your children rooted in God?

The College Scene: A Rite of Passage

Only God is the Lord of your conscience when it comes to the education of your children. There is no biblical law against sending your child to the typical American college. But, you do need to think about the college issue and not mindlessly float down stream with the cultural tide. There are stark realities, biblical principles, and practical alternatives that God would at least have you consider.

One of the most dangerous places for children is college. Think about children in that context. Most teens including Christians have no biblical worldview, little if any judgment, virtually no life experience, no practical wisdom, and raging hormones. Add to that peer pressure, co-ed dorms, fraternity mixers, and a culture that literally expects them to have a four year party with all the trappings of sex, drugs, and alcohol. In fact, the college scene has become a rite of passage in America. Do you really expect your children, saved or not, to come through without falling in some way in that environment? According to the Scriptures, even a spiritually mature and committed Christian adult would be unwise to place himself in the midst of that kind of temptation. It is amazing to see parents who have done a great job of protecting their children send them off to the unprotected environment of college when a young adult is the most vulnerable for temptation.

What is even more amazing is that families will pay on average of $64,000 for a public college and over $132,000 for a private college to obtain a bachelor's degree. Many of these families go into massive debt for the privilege of having the institution destroy their child's belief in God! Not only are all the wolves lurking on campus, but the young adult is immersed in a culture that exudes the exact opposite of their Christian values. This is the "straw that breaks the camel's back" with respect to the nearly ninety percent of our children that we are losing from the church.

There are a number of alternatives available for the parent who chooses formal education but wants to protect her children. As we consider the way that Jesus made disciples, here they are from best to worst.

- Christian Distance Learning- Fully accredited Christian colleges that allow students to earn their degree from the safety and comfort of their homes.
- Distance Learning- The same as above, except the student is acquiring a non-biblical education. Parents would be wise to screen curriculums and point out error. Distance learning is the lowest cost and lowest time investment approach to getting a college education. Some students have earned fully-accredited Bachelor Degrees in six months time and less than $5,000 in total costs! Students can start earning college credits before they graduate from high school.
- Off Campus Christian College- The student attends classes at a local Christian college, but lives at home. There are increased costs, time and exposure to wolves, such as peers and some teachers.
- Off Campus Secular College- Same as above, but students are acquiring a non-biblical education. Many wolves exist in this environment, but at least the student lives at home. You will need to work hard to repair the damage done by secular education.
- On Campus Christian College- This option is slightly better than on Campus Secular College.
- On Campus Secular College- This is the worst possible option. A parent can do little to protect his child in this environment.

There is an excellent ministry available to families called *CollegePlus!*. The ministry coaches families through the distance learning process. Their trained coaches are able to help a student select the appropriate college, develop a degree plan, and improve learning skills. The coaches stay in touch with the students to keep them on track with their educational goals. This moderate financial investment ultimately saves a lot of time and money.

Again, remember your goals when it comes to your children. Those goals must be rooted in God and they may or may not be at odds with His revealed will. That is for you to decide.

Dating

Sexual activity among teens is something every Christian parent fears with good reason. Bristol Palin, eighteen year old daughter of Alaska Governor Sarah Palin, shocked Christians once again after the election when she said that even though teens should not have sex, abstinence is "not realistic at all." Most of us cringe at such a statement. Yet, in some sense, she is actually right.

Consider these comments from Dr. Albert Mohler, President of Southern Baptist Theological Seminary:

Is sexual abstinence realistic for teenagers and young adults? Well, abstinence is certainly not realistic when teenagers put themselves - or they are put there by others - into a situation where sexual activity is likely. . . .The real issue for Christian teenagers and their parents is not to debate whether sexual abstinence before marriage is realistic or not. The larger and more important issue is that sexual abstinence until marriage is the biblical expectation and command. Once this is realized, the responsibility for everyone concerned is to ensure that expectations and structures are in place so that abstinence is realistic. The debate over whether abstinence is realistic or not misses the more important issue — abstinence must be made realistic. Parents and teenagers must make certain that adequate protections and expectations are in place so that sexual abstinence is very realistic indeed. Far too many Christian parents allow their teenagers to be part of the "hooking up" scene of teenage culture. In that highly sexualized context, sexual abstinence would appear unrealistic in the extreme. Premature pair dating and unsupervised liaisons, set within the supercharged culture of teenage sexuality, can put teenagers into very vulnerable situations. . . .But, the real issue here is our responsibility to ensure that abstinence is made realistic and stays realistic. Anything short of this is truly "not realistic at all."[27]

Mohler is calling on parents to protect their children and thereby make abstinence realistic.

The reality is that men and women are created to be attracted to one another. This attraction is God's design. Add to that design our sinful nature, our sexually-charged culture, teens that lack judgment and experience placed in the way of temptation, and one has little hope that most will be able to withstand the pressure placed upon them. If you put candy in front of a baby it is unrealistic to expect him not to take it at some point.

The modern day practice of dating has yielded terrible results. More than fifty percent of all Christian marriages end in divorce; this statistic is slightly worse than the world. The majority of Christian children have lost their sexual purity before they are married according to Barna Research. This bitter fruit points to a sick tree. The only good news is the fact that the church is doing slightly better than the world. Ninety-five percent of all Americans (Christians and non-Christians) have lost their purity before marriage. Of course Scripture commands us to do otherwise. "Flee sexual immorality. Every sin that a man does is outside the body, but he who commits sexual immorality sins against his own body" (1 Corinthians 6:18).

Since dating has been the norm for a long time, most of us who are parents also dated. But, is the practice really biblical? How can a young person find a mate without dating? Is there a satisfying alternative?

If you think about the experience that we get when we date it would include the following:

- We learn how to flirt, to lust, and to get dates with members of the opposite sex.
- We learn how to get intimate at various levels and 95 percent go all the way.
- We learn how to break up when we find someone who seems more attractive; we learn how to hurt others, to break hearts, and then move on to the next person.

Is there anything biblical about learning these things? Scripture tells us to love one another. "Since you have purified your souls in obeying the truth through the Spirit in sincere love of the brethren, love one another fervently with a pure heart" (1 Peter 1:22).

> "…we learn how to hurt others, to break hearts, and then move on to the next person."

How does this training influence young adults after marriage? They have learned how to flirt, get dates, and seduce; these well trained experts naturally continue their habits after marriage. Becoming intimate with strangers is all too easy and breaking up with your spouse is relatively easy because you have done this many times in your dating experiences. After all, half of your friends are becoming divorced as well.

Parents, would you trust yourself to go on a date with an attractive and willing person of the opposite sex? Would you trust your spouse to do the same? Paul gives us the answer by way of warning in 1 Corinthians 10:12: "Let him who thinks he stands, take heed lest he fall." Why would you expect that your teenager or young adult should be able to resist that temptation when boys are at their sexual peak and when ninety-five percent of all youth are losing their sexual purity before marriage?

There are a number of biblical reasons that your children should remain sexually pure. The Song of Solomon tells us that love should not be aroused before its time (2:7). The Bible speaks of the virtuous woman. "Who can find a virtuous wife? For her worth is far above rubies. The heart of her husband safely trusts her; so he will have no lack of gain. She does him good and not evil all the days of her life" (Proverbs 31:10-12). If a young woman has sex with other men before marriage she is not doing her future husband good. She will have memories of these sexual encounters after she is married. She may compare her husband to her past sexual experiences. If she makes contact with a former boyfriend she may be tempted to see him again. The same is true of the young man who has had a number of sexual partners. He may fantasize about these encounters and be tempted to seek out an old girlfriend in the future.

Further, Scripture commands us to not defraud others.

For this is the will of God, your sanctification: that you should abstain from sexual immorality; that each of you should know how to possess his own vessel in sanctification and honor, not in passion of lust, like the Gentiles who do not know God; that no one should take advantage of and defraud his brother in this matter, because the Lord is the avenger of all such, as we also forewarned you and testified. For God did not call us to uncleanness, but in holiness (1 Thessalonians 4:3-7).

Boys and girls who have sex outside of marriage are defrauding one another.

Think of the physical dangers in dating. Date rape is an increasing threat. Of course, premarital sex will make your child vulnerable to sexually transmitted diseases and out of wedlock pregnancies. Abortion will be a temptation, maybe even without your knowledge.

Dating is a dangerous choice because it will cause your child to lust and be tempted to sin. Most will lose their virginity, they will defraud one another when they break up, they will hurt others, they may marry non-believers, and it will make their marriages more likely to end in divorce.

Consider Biblical Alternatives

If dating is not biblical, what is the alternative? Deciding on a marriage partner will be the most important decision that your children make in life. Hopefully they will spend the rest of their lives with a person who will be a great blessing. But they may spend the rest of their lives with a person who is a great curse. Or they may spend the rest of their lives with several persons, married or not, constantly looking for the perfect companion.

Paul told Timothy, "Do not rebuke an older man, but exhort him as a father, younger men as brothers, older women as mothers, younger as sisters, with all purity" (1 Timothy 5:1-2). Timothy and other young men are commanded here to think of younger women as sisters, with all purity. Jesus told us that lust is the same as committing adultery. A young man must pray that God would lead him to his future wife. He must determine boundaries he will not cross. He must keep his feelings in check and follow biblical wisdom in his relationships with young women. Of course, young women must do exactly the same thing when it comes to themselves and young men.

The key is to view love from a biblical perspective. Love is not about feelings or physical attraction though the marital relationship certainly has those things. In our culture, typically a man and a woman will be physically attracted to one another and begin a dating relationship. That relationship may include physical intimacy of one kind or another. The Bible calls this *eros*. When a relationship is built on *eros*, not only is such improper outside of marriage, it is the weakest foundation where couples are concerned. The dating relationship may progress to another level where the couple actually become friends and have genuine affection for one another (*phileo*). Marriage may be the ultimate result and the couple will get along fine until trouble starts. Because they have no real, biblical love for one another (*agape*), their feelings of affection wane and they simply believe they are no longer in love. *Eros* is not enough to sustain the relationship and divorce ensues.

For any marriage to last, it must be built upon the foundation of *agape*. Such love is a decision of the will. It is a commitment to love someone no matter what for the glory of God and the good of that someone. It involves sacrifice and service and is not contingent upon circumstances or feelings. Those things will change often. *Agape* will not. And, when a marriage is built upon *agape*, affection (*phileo*) and intimacy (*eros*) will be present.

The implication for young men and women is that one does not have to be ruled by feelings or physical attraction.

One can make wise decisions under the leadership of the Holy Spirit. One can avoid being ensnared by runaway feelings and temptation. Young people can be patient and wait for God to bring the right person into their lives.

Marriage can be viewed as something wonderful but not an arena for one's personal fulfillment. It is an arena for God's glory. The same is true of any relationship outside of marriage. Thus, young men and women need not date. They need not pursue personal fulfillment. They can delight in pursuing God's glory. One can focus on God and others and not self in this context.

"Both boys and girls will guard their hearts."

You may be thinking, "So far, so good. But, how do young people get married if they don't date?" While many scenarios could be offered, stay focused on the principles. Boys and girls will meet in a variety of contexts. In God's providence, a young man may enjoy a particular young woman's company. If they have been discipled, they will get help from the Lord, their parents, and one another to keep their relationship where it needs to be: at a friendship level only. Both boys and girls will guard their hearts. They will remember to live for God's glory and not themselves. Their parents will be involved and biblical wisdom will guide. If all is well and they continue to enjoy each other's company, again, with their parents' involvement, they can spend some time together to see what God does. They will continue to make every effort to guard their hearts and indeed their purity. *Agape* will be the focus. God may then lead them to be engaged and later married. With God at the center, their relationship will only get better over time.

Is such a thing realistic? I've officiated at more than one wedding where the bride and groom kissed each other for the very first time at the altar. You talk about a celebration of

God and of married love! Among other things, think of the gift these couples have to give one another. Don't you want that for your children? You bet it's realistic.

What I've described above has no label. I've not given a legalistic code. Again, God Himself is Lord of your conscience. What I've described above is just an application of biblical principles.

An old but now increasingly popular form of what I've described above is called "courtship." In some circles the concept is pretty rigid and in others not so rigid. Josh Harris' books *I Kissed Dating Goodbye* and *Boy Meets Girl: Say Hello to Courtship* are variants on this theme and are extremely popular among young Christians.[28] These resources may be helpful to you, they may not be.

As always, the issue before us is to think, and to think biblically. When we do, we will constantly evaluate what we are doing and pray about what we should do. If we would disciple our children for God's glory and their good, we will give all of these things prayerful consideration. We will, with the Lord's help, make the best decision we can for our families.

Chapter Sixteen

Send Them Out — Armed!

There will come a point in time when your children will marry and move out. Then, not only will they leave you but they will cleave to their spouses (Matthew 19:5). That does not mean that you cannot be involved in their lives. On the contrary, as noted, you should enjoy a life-long relationship of joy with your children. It does mean that they will have their own families though. It does mean that they will have been trained by you to disciple their children like Jesus. And, it does mean that like Jesus, you will send them out. Remember, Jesus said He would be with us in the power of the Spirit. Because of that, we are to make disciples of all the nations. We are to be witnesses as we go. You must spend your parenting years training and preparing your children (and yourself) for the day you will send them out. And, when you send them out, again, it will be for the glory of God and the advance of the gospel.

Send your Children Out

All true Christians become familiar with the Great Commission early in their spiritual lives. At the same time, there is another mandate in the Scriptures that is equally massive in terms of obligation and resulting implications: the dominion mandate of Genesis 1:28. Further, we are told by our Lord to be salt and light that men might see our good works and glorify our Father in heaven (Matthew 5:13-16). Certainly these directives are interconnected and are all grounded in the gospel of Jesus Christ. Yet, few believers understand the profound duty placed upon us in these areas. Neither do we realize the consequences for that failure of understanding. A large number of Christians shrink away from thinking about culture or seeing any responsibility placed upon them concerning cultural influence. Just what does it mean to be in the world but not of the world? While such influence must be accomplished in every sphere of our cultural context from the arts, to the markets, to the entertainment industry, to the sciences, to the political arena, etc., precious few see the necessity of such engagement or even care. A failure to see in this regard is the sure pathway to the marginalization and then ban of Christianity. In short, we must involve ourselves in cultural engagement.

Only committed followers of Christ will attempt such. They will understand that God has called them not to isolate themselves, but to go into the world and make a difference for Christ.

Parents, disciple your children like Jesus and then send them out, armed, because kingdom advance is why we're here. There are two competing kingdoms in this world, God's and Satan's; though they are not on equal footing. Certainly God is sovereign over all things. Yet, He has chosen, through the person and work of Christ, to advance His kingdom and that primarily through the influence of believers. He uses us to put His enemies under His feet through the preaching of the gospel (1 Corinthians 15:25). If we fail to do so, the Kingdom of Satan continues to encroach upon the Kingdom of God in the world.

For example, the Kingdom of Darkness encroaches in regard to our biggest social issues. Simply consider a few of the massive concerns before us in this culture: abortion, euthanasia, cloning, the homosexual agenda, etc. Pharmacists are required in some places to dispense the morning after pill even if it violates their consciences. In these citations alone the moral breakdown of our culture combined with the erosion of personal liberty has served to advance evil in our society in an unprecedented way.

Further, the Kingdom of Darkness encroaches in regard to our deepest philosophical commitments. One need only cite the dynamics of political correctness, postmodernism, hate speech legislation, and the like to sound the alarm. If the tide is not turned, a day is fast approaching when the gospel itself will be banned in this country.

Perhaps the most chilling implication is that the Kingdom of Darkness encroaches in regard to our prized treasure: our children. A moral agenda vastly different from the average Christian's has taken hold in the land. Biblical values are out while evolution, socialism, and homosexuality are in. If you disciple your children like Jesus, they will be protected. You will then want to send them out to influence other parents to disciple their children.

Now, we are here to encroach on Satan's kingdom with the power of Christ in the gospel of grace. Of course, we are not talking about forced Christianity. At issue here is gospel advance for the salvation of souls, the glory of God, and the betterment of the lives of all people in the society in which God has placed us. The betterment of the lives of others is implied in the preserving influence we have as the salt of the earth. Further, the Lord Jesus said, "I will build my church and the gates of Hell will not prevail against it" (Matthew 16:18). The picture here is that of the church advancing even as the gates of Hell attempt to hold that Kingdom from encroaching into its (so-called) territory. Those gates cannot keep Christ from accomplishing His purpose.

Again, in part, Christ accomplishes His purpose through us as He has given us a commission to make disciples of all nations. If we cannot see the degeneration of depraved man all around us and the need for gospel advance, then indeed we are the ones who are blind. At the same time, if we cannot affirm the power of Christ and His gospel and go forth with confidence then we do not understand who we are or what we have in the gospel. A definition of evangelism I've embraced and taught over the years is quite simple: "Being, doing, and telling the gospel of the Kingdom of God in order that, by the power of the Holy Spirit, persons and structures may be converted to the lordship of Jesus Christ." Note the kingdom emphasis: "the gospel of the Kingdom of God." The only way for persons and structures to be converted to the lordship of Christ is for God's people to engage those persons and structures. You and your children must engage.

Parents, disciple your children like Jesus and then send them out, armed, because God deserves glory in every sphere. In the definition of evangelism cited above, not only are persons to be converted to the lordship of Christ but so too are structures. Of course, we could add the fact that ideas are to be converted as well. Paul noted,

> For though we walk in the flesh, we do not war according to the flesh. For the weapons of our warfare are not carnal but mighty in God for pulling down strongholds, casting down arguments and every high thing that exalts itself against the knowledge of God, bringing every thought into captivity to the obedience of Christ (2 Corinthians 10:3-5).

If God deserves glory in every sphere, then He is to be acknowledged in every sphere. Such a truth has great implications for prayer from a Christian at the opening of a football game or council meeting. Further, if God deserves glory in every sphere, then He is to be influential in every sphere. Of course God has influence in those spheres in which His people are engaged: hence the need for cultural engagement.

Parents, disciple your children like Jesus and then send them out, armed, because Christians are misguided in their approach. Some Christians understand the need of the hour and are engaging the culture. The problem lies in the fact that they are taking the wrong tack. Christ Himself said, "My kingdom is not of this world. If My kingdom were of this world, My servants would fight, so that I should not be delivered to the Jews; but now My kingdom is not from here" (John 18:36). Christ is not building a physical kingdom but a spiritual one.

Many Christians have the wrong goal when it comes to cultural engagement. Too often the goal is a mere moral nation through government coercion. Or, too often the goal is a completely Christian nation through government coercion. Dr. Tom Nettles once said to me, "We glory in a pluralistic society." Did he say that because he is a pluralist or because he did not want souls to be saved? No. He made such a statement because we cannot force anyone to be a Christian nor do we have the right to make such an attempt. Not only is the Holy Spirit the only One who can accomplish such a transformation but the New Testament advocates freedom for all human beings. People have the freedom to be wrong about whom God is.

Other Christians are wrong in their method. While Christians must be active in the political arena, they must never come to believe that politics or government can or will change the world. We want Christian influence in the public square but such influence must always be connected to the lordship of Christ and the exposition of the gospel in that context. At the same time, co-belligerence, that is, partnering with those of other faiths for social change will not do in this effort. Our efforts in regard to social issues must never be divorced from the gospel we believe. Partnering with unbelievers even for a good cause will necessarily compromise the gospel we must preach in that framework.

So, we must engage the culture. Part of that requires that we point out to our brothers and sisters in Christ the error of their approach and do it right for the sake of our Lord Jesus Christ.

Parents, disciple your children like Jesus and then send them out, armed, because they need not waste their lives, or even part of their lives. A major problem, even in biblically sound churches today, is that the vast majority of individuals are focused on themselves rather than kingdom advance. The pursuit of the American Dream supersedes pursuit of the gospel. We need a fresh understanding of why God put us here and the reward we stand to gain on that great day.

Don't waste your life! At the end of your days, you will not regret the things you did but you will most certainly regret the things you did not do. This reality will hold true with particular reference to what you do or do not do for the sake of kingdom advance if you are a true believer. Paul wrote, "See then that ye walk circumspectly, not as fools, but as wise, redeeming the time, because the days are evil. Therefore do not be unwise, but understand what the will of the Lord is" (Ephesians 5:15-17).

Your Children will be Armed!

If you disciple your children like Jesus, you can send them out because they will be armed to the teeth with the truth. When they go forth with the gospel to others, they will not go forth with empty hands. They will go forth with the Word, the power, the Spirit, and the assurance of God (1 Thessalonians 1:5). Further, they can go forth with an expectation of results. It is the gospel message that produces in people powerful change, spiritual joy, holy living, gospel proclamation, eternal salvation, and eternal hope among other things (1:5-10).

Like Paul, your children will not minister in vain. He told the Thessalonians: "For you yourselves know, brethren, that our coming to you was not in vain" (2:1). Your children will not go forth empty-handed. They will be equipped to give rather than to receive. Through them God will change lives. People will turn from idols to serve the Living God (1:9). What better encouragement to take the gospel to others can anyone offer?

When you disciple your children like Jesus, you will be able to send them out because they will be bold in their witness for Christ. They will be such despite potential suffering or persecution. If they are followers of Christ, you can count on Him to give them courage in a rough and tumble world.

God will give your children more than courage. He will be with them and help them! You can trust Him. Boldness comes from God and it is the Lord God Almighty who enables us to speak despite great difficulty. Read how Paul puts it on another occasion:

> For these reasons the Jews seized me in the temple and tried to kill me. Therefore, having obtained help from God, to this day I stand, witnessing both to small and great, saying no other things than those which the prophets and Moses said would come — that the Christ would suffer, that He would be the first to rise from the dead, and would proclaim light to the Jewish people and to the Gentiles (Acts 26:21-23).

Paul continued to witness the gospel having obtained help from God. So too will your children if they are following Christ.

If you disciple your children like Jesus, you can send them out because they will be consummate examples to others. In a day of complacency in the church, they will spread the word of God. They will be like the ordinary believers at Thessalonica: "For from you the word of the Lord has sounded forth, not only in Macedonia and Achaia, but also in every place" (1 Thessalonians 1:8). Followers of Christ will make disciples of others. This is what you want for your children. You want the gospel to spread far and wide as a result of their faithful witness.

As a result, your children will be known as followers of Christ (for His glory). Again, the change wrought in their lives will so amaze others that they won't be able to help but speak of that change and give glory to God.

If your children follow Jesus, no one will have to defend their actions for no one will be able to lay a charge against them. They will be like Daniel in that sense. Those who hated him had to lay a trap for him because he was faithful to God and man. Wolves will seek to undermine the credibility of your adult children as they are bold for Christ. But, the lives they lead, the ministry they render, and the God they serve will be their defense.

You can be confident in the future as you disciple like Jesus now. Your children will constantly deal with idols in their hearts as you will have trained them to do so. They will faithfully serve the one true and living God because you will have trained them to do so.

Send your children out! They will cling to what is good and live their lives in such a way that others will see God in them. They will attempt great things for God because they will expect great things from God. They will have peace and hope that unbelievers do not have. They will have the assurance that Christ is one day coming again.

Appendix

What to do to protect your children

In summary, there are many types of wolves that may threaten your children. Here are some things you can do to protect your children. Since Jesus protected His adult disciples, these principles are appropriate for children of all ages until they are on their own.

- Confess your own sins and turn away from them.
- Ask the Lord to open your eyes to the dangers that your children face.
- Keep your children in your presence; this is the greatest protection you can provide.
- Monitor your child's activities.
- Take your children into the world for ministry, but don't immerse them in regular ungodly activities.
- Protect your children through training and discipline.
- Protect your children by teaching them what is good and what is evil.

- Warn your children about wolves; philosophical, moral, technology, entertainment and predator wolves.
- Install internet filters. Don't let your children visit chat rooms.
- Unsubscribe from cable television and use carefully selected videos for viewing. For a lower level of protection, subscribe to Sky Angel or other television filtering. Limit commercial advertising, since many commercials promote sex and non-biblical worldviews.
- Place computers and televisions in a public area of your home, such as the family room. Remove them from children's rooms.
- When children are with their peers, keep them in your presence.
- Like Jesus, when out in public, go with other trusted adults. Always be aware of your surroundings and people that could be a threat.
- Rather than frequenting malls, shop online. Malls have all kinds of temptations and threats to families.
- If you must send them into the world without your protection, send them out with a trusted Christian adult that you know well. Pray for your children diligently.

Notes

1. SBC.net, Jon Walker, "Family Life Council Says it's Time to bring Family Back to Life," 2002 SBC Annual Meeting, http://www.sbcannualmeeting.net/sbc02/newsroom/newspage.asp?ID=261, June 12, 2002. (Further, this information is based on US Government Census data (http://www.census.gov/main/www/popclock.html) that shows the total US Population of approximately 300 million. According to Pew research approximately 70% identified as Christians (http://religions.pewforum.org/reports). This calculates to approximately 210 million Christians. Approximately 20% of the population is age 5-19, or 42 million Christian students. Over 14 years the average number of Christian students amounts to approximately 3 million children at each grade level. Assuming that we are only losing 75% (which is at the lower end of various studies), this amounts to a loss of over 2 million children each year by their 2nd year of college.

2. C. S. Lewis, *The Screwtape Letters* (New York: HarperOne, 2001).

3. Alan Jones, *Reimagining Christianity* (Hoboken: Wiley, 2004), 31.

4. Jay Younts, *Everyday Talk: Talking Freely and Naturally about God with Your Children* (Wapwallopen: Shepherd Press, 2004).

5. "Teenagers Spend an Average of 31 Hours Online" *Telegraph.co.uk*, February 13, 2009, Technology section, http://www.telegraph.co.uk/scienceandtechnology/technology/4574792/Teenagers-spend-an-average-of-31-hours-online.html.

6. John Piper has elaborated extensively on the glory of God as the motivation for the Christian life and has perhaps more than any twenty-first century theologian demonstrated the primary way to glorify God is to enjoy Him. Piper has summarized the essence of his thought in this phrase, "God is most glorified in us when we are most satisfied in Him." For a fuller treatment of this subject, see his various resource offerings online at www.desiringgod.org.

7. Honora Gathings, "Increasing Self Esteem, Decreasing Violence," ABC News Affiliate Birmingham AL, September 21, 2008, Read section, http://www.abc3340.com/news/stories/0908/555298.html.

8. Crosswalk.com, Jeremy Lelek, "Do Children Need a High Self-Esteem?" http://www.crosswalk.com/11581096/.

9. AFP, "Poll Says Materialistic Society is Damaging Children," http://afp.google.com/article/ALeqM5gS8-F5eLWncNOl-oD4EiFJSKuAvQ, February 26, 2008.

10. Hillary Clinton, *It Takes a Village* (New York: Simon & Schuster, 1996).

11. Charles Sheldon, *In His Steps* (Grand Rapids: Revell, 1994).

12. John MacArthur, *The Book on Leadership* (Nashville: Thomas Nelson, 2004).

13. Barna Group, "The Spirituality of Moms Outpaces that of Dads," May 7, 2007, http://barna.org/barna-update/article/15-familykids/104-the-spirituality-of-moms-outpaces-that-of-dads.

14. Exploring Homeschooling, "About Exploring Homeschooling," http://www.exploringhomeschooling.com/AboutExploringHomeschooling.aspx.

15. http://www.visionforum.com/hottopics/blogs/dwp/

16. Harry Chapin, "Cat's in the Cradle," Elektra Records, 1974.

17. WorldNetDaily, "Father Spanks Daughter at High School," http://www.worldnetdaily.com/news/article.asp?ARTICLE_ID=37287, February 5, 2004.

18. Ibid.

19. Jay Adams is credited with being the primary catalyst for the church's rediscovery of the discipline of Biblical Counseling. For a fuller treatment of habituation, the biblical concept of put off and put on, see his various resource offerings online at www.nouthetic.org.

20. For a fuller treatment of feeling, doing, and heart levels, see John Broger's *Self-Confrontation: A Manual for in-depth*

Discipleship and other resources online at www.bcfminis-tries.org.

21. Arnold Pent, *Ten P's in a Pod: A Million Mile Journal of the Arnold Pent Family* (San Antonio: The Vision Forum, Inc., 2004).

22. Safe Families, "Statistics on Pornography, Sexual Addiction and Online Perpetrators," http://www.safefami-lies.org/sfStats.php.

23. CBS News, "Study Links Sex on TV to Teen Pregnancy," November 3, 2008, http://www.cbsnews.com/stories/2008/11/03/health/main4564612.shtml?source=related_story.

24. P2P Net, "Violence in the Media and Teen Violence," http://www.p2pnet.net/story/17729.

25. Born to Fly International, http://born2fly.org/index_working.html.

26. The Henry Institute, Russell D. Moore, "Does Your Child's Cell Phone Preach Another Gospel?" February 9th, 2009, http://www.russellmoore.com/index.php/2009/02/09/does-your-childs-cell-phone-preach-another-gospel/.

27. Albert Mohler, "The Palin Parable — Bristol Says Abstinence 'Not Realistic At All,'" February 19, 2009, http://albertmohler.com/blog_read.php?id=3319.

28. Josh Harris, *I Kissed Dating Goodbye* (Sisters: Multnomah, 2003) and *Boy Meets Girl: Say Hello to Courtship* (Sisters: Multnomah, 2005).

Other Resources From Disciple Like Jesus

Disciple Like Jesus For Parents Study Guide

Are you ready to disciple like Jesus? This 16 unit study guide will lead an individual parent or a group through the process of assessing how you are presently training your children and what steps you can take to better follow Jesus. This practical study guide is the companion to *Disciple Like Jesus For Parents*. This resource is for the serious parent who wants follow the approach that Jesus personally used. Implement the Lord's approach and watch Him transform your family into the image of Christ, and enjoy the great blessings of children.

This resource will be available in summer 2009.

Disciple Like Jesus For Church Leaders

Are you a church leader and are ready to equip your congregation to disciple like Jesus? Church leaders will model the discipleship practices of Jesus and teach their flock how to follow Jesus in His method. *Disciple Like Jesus* ministry has created a strong demand from pastors and ministry leaders for a practical resource that can be used to implement the discipleship practices of Jesus Christ. This book will provide practical helps to get you started. Your church members will experience spiritual growth like you never have witnessed!

This book will be available in early 2010.

For more information, visit www.DiscipleLikeJesus.com or call 864.895.8008.

About the Authors

Alan Melton is the founder of Disciple Like Jesus ministry. The ministry encourages parents and grandparents to disciple their children in the same manner that Jesus made disciples. His articles have been featured in numerous publications, and he speaks at churches, associations and conferences. Alan has served the Lord as a church planter, teaching elder, deacon chairman and business owner. He led Evangelism Explosion and FAITH evangelism training ministries for 10 years and juvenile delinquent ministries for 16 years. Married to Donna since 1977, he has two children, Jennifer and Ryan.

Paul J. Dean is the pastor of Providence Baptist Church in Greer, SC. He is a graduate of New Orleans Baptist Theological Seminary (M.Div., Th.M.) and Erskine Theological Seminary (D.Min.). Dr. Dean is also a Regional Mentor with the International Association of Biblical Counselors. He speaks at several conferences throughout the year, provides training for ministers and churches on a regular basis in the area of counseling and discipleship, and hosts a live, call-in, radio talk show: "Calling for Truth." He is married and has three children.